College World Series Record Book
1947-2002

ISBN 0-9645819-4-9 (Paperback)

Library of Congress Number: 2003091309

Printed in the United States of America. Information for this book provided with permission from the NCAA.

Madden Publishing Company, Inc.
10872 Washington Bay Drive
Fishers, IN 46038
317-842-9856

Cover Photo
Columbus State Cougar players celebrate after winning the Division II College World Series in 2002. (Photo courtesy of Mike Peacock and Columbus State.)

Back Cover Photo
Texas Longhorn players hold up the NCAA trophy plaque after winning the Division I College World Series in 2002. (Photo by W.C. Madden)

Contents

Division I 4
    Division I Results, 1947-2002 6
    Most Outstanding Player Award 7
    Division I World Series Results 8
    Boxscores from National Championship Finals 18
    All-Time Won-Lost Record (1947-2002) 51
    World Series Sites 53
    Division I Records 54
    Series Records 59
    Career Records 63
    Championship Game Records 65
    All-Time Teams 73
    All-Time Coaching Records By School 75
    The Last Time 82
    National Championship Totals 83
Division II 84
    Division II Results, 1968-2002 86
    Most Outstanding Player Award 86
    Division II Records 87
    Boxscore for National Championship Final 2002 90
    National Championship Totals 91
    World Series Sites 91
Division III 92
    Division III Results, 1976-2002 94
    Most Outstanding Player Award 94
    Division III Records 95
    World Series Sites 97
    Boxscore for National Championship Final 2002 98
    National Championship Totals 99
Survey 100

Cover to the program for the first College World Series.

The College World Series Record Book

Division I Records

Division I Results, 1947-2002

Year	Champion (Record)	Coach	Score	Runner-up
1947	California (31-10)	Clint Evans	8-7	Yale
1948	Southern Cal (26-4)	Sam Barry	9-2	Yale
1949	Texas (23-7)	Bibb Falk	10-3	Wake Forest
1950	Texas (27-6)	Bibb Falk	3-0	Washington St.
1951	Oklahoma (19-9)	Jack Baer	3-2	Tennessee
1952	Holy Cross (21-3)	Jack Barry	8-4	Missouri
1953	Michigan (21-9)	Ray Fisher	7-5	Texas
1954	Missouri (22-4)	John Simmons	4-1	Rollins
1955	Wake Forest (29-7)	Taylor Sanford	7-6	Western Michigan
1956	Minnesota (37-9)	Dick Siebert	12-1	Arizona
1957	California (35-10)	George Wolfman	1-0	Penn St.
1958	Southern Cal (29-3)	Rod Dedeaux	8-7	Missouri
1959	Oklahoma State (27-5)	Toby Greene	5-3	Arizona
1960	Minnesota (34-7-1)	Dick Siebert	2-1	Southern Cal
1961	Southern Cal (36-7)	Rod Dedeaux	1-0	Oklahoma St.
1962	Michigan (34-15)	Don Lund	5-4	Santa Clara
1963	Southern Cal (35-10)	Rod Dedeaux	5-2	Arizona
1964	Minnesota (31-12)	Dick Siebert	5-1	Missouri
1965	Arizona State (53-8)	Bobby Winkles	2-1	Ohio St.
1966	Ohio State (27-6-1)	Marty Karow	8-2	Oklahoma St.
1967	Arizona State (53-12)	Bobby Winkles	11-2	Houston
1968	Southern Cal (43-12-1)	Rod Dedeaux	4-3	Southern Illinois
1969	Arizona State (56-11)	Bobby Winkles	10-1	Tulsa
1970	Southern Cal (45-13)	Rod Dedeaux	2-1	Florida St.
1971	Southern Cal (46-11)	Rod Dedeaux	7-2	Southern Illinois
1972	Southern Cal (47-13-1)	Rod Dedeaux	1-0	Arizona St.
1973	Southern Cal (51-11)	Rod Dedeaux	4-3	Arizona St.
1974	Southern Cal (50-20)	Rod Dedeaux	7-3	Miami (Fla.)
1975	Texas (59-6)	Cliff Gustafson	5-1	South Carolina
1976	Arizona (56-17)	Jerry Kindall	7-1	Eastern Michigan
1977	Arizona State (57-12)	Jim Brock	2-1	South Carolina
1978	Southern Cal (54-9)	Rod Dedeaux	10-3	Arizona St.
1979	Cal St. Fullerton (60-14-1)	Augie Garrido	2-1	Arkansas
1980	Arizona (45-21-1)	Jerry Kindall	5-3	Hawaii
1981	Arizona State (55-13)	Jim Brock	7-4	Oklahoma St.
1982	Miami (Fla.) (55-17-1)	Ron Fraser	9-3	Wichita St.
1983	Texas (66-14)	Cliff Gustafson	4-3	Alabama
1984	Cal St. Fullerton (66-20)	Augie Garrido	3-1	Texas
1985	Miami (Fla.) (64-16)	Ron Fraser	10-6	Texas
1986	Arizona (49-19)	Jerry Kindall	10-2	Florida St.
1987	Stanford (53-17)	Mark Marquess	9-5	Oklahoma St
1988	Stanford (46-23)	Mark Marquess	9-4	Arizona St.
1989	Wichita St. (68-16)	Gene Stephenson	5-3	Texas

1990	Georgia (52-19)	Steve Webber	2-1	Oklahoma St.
1991	LSU (55-18)	Skip Bertman	6-3	Wichita St.
1992	Pepperdine (48-11-1)	Andy Lopez	3-2	Cal St. Fullerton
1993	LSU (53-17-1)	Skip Bertman	8-0	Wichita St.
1994	Oklahoma (50-17)	Larry Cochell	13-5	Georgia Tech
1995	Cal St. Fullerton (57-9)	Augie Garrido	11-5	Southern Cal
1996	LSU (52-15)	Skip Bertman	9-8	Miami (Fla.)
1997	LSU (57-13)	Skip Bertman	13-6	Alabama
1998	Southern Cal (49-17)	Mike Gillespie	21-14	Arizona St.
1999	Miami (Fla.) (50-13)	Jim Morris	6-5	Florida St.
2000	LSU (52-17)	Skip Bertram	6-5	Stanford
2001	Miami (Fla.) (53-12)	Jim Morris	12-1	Stanford
2002	Texas (57-15)	Augie Garrido	12-6	South Carolina

Most Outstanding Player Award

1949 - Charles Teague, Texas, 2b
1950 - Ray VanCleef, Rutgers, of
1951 - Sidney Hatfield, Tenn., 1b-p
1952 - James O'Neill, Holy Cross, p
1953 - J.L. Smith, Texas, p
1954 - Tom Yewcic, Michigan St., c
1955 - Tom Borland, Okla. St., p
1956 - Jerry Thomas, Minn., p
1957 - Cal Emery, Penn St., 1b-p
1958 - Bill Thom, Southern Cal, p
1959 - Jim Dodson, Okla. St., 3b
1960 - John Erickson, Minn., 2b
1961 - Littleton Fowler, Okla. St., p
1962 - Bob Garibaldi, Santa Clara, p
1963 - Bud Hollowell, Southern Cal, c
1964 - Joe Ferris, Maine, p
1965 - Sal Bando, Arizona St., 3b
1966 - Steve Arlin, Ohio St., p
1967 - Ron Davini, Arizona St., of
1968 - Bill Seinsoth, Southern Cal, 1b
1969 - John Dolinsek, Arizona St., of
1970 - Gene Ammann, Florida St., p
1971 - Jerry Tabb, Tulsa, 1b
1972 - Russ McQueen, Southern Cal, p
1973 - Dave Winfield, Minn., p-of
1974 - George Milke, Southern Cal, p
1975 - Mickey Reichenbach, Texas, 1b
1976 - Steve Powers, Arizona, dh-p
1977 - Bob Horner, Arizona St., 2b
1978 - Rod Boxberger, Southern Cal, p
1979 - Tony Hudson, Cal St. Ful., p
1980 - Terry Francona, Arizona, of
1981 - Stan Holmes, Arizona St., of
1982 - Dan Smith, Miami (Fla.), p
1983 - Calvin Schiraldi, Texas, p
1984 - John Fishel, Cal St. Fullerton., of
1985 - Greg Ellena, Miami (Fla.), dh
1986 - Mike Senne, Arizona, of
1987 - Paul Carey, Stanford, of
1988 - Lee Plemel, Stanford, p
1989 - Greg Brummett, Wichita St., p
1990 - Mike Rebhan, Georgia, p
1991 - Gary Hymel, LSU, c
1992 - Phil Nevin, Cal St. Ful., 3b
1993 - Todd Walker, LSU, 2b
1994 - Chip Glass, Oklahoma, of
1995 - Mark Kotsay, Cal St. Ful., of-p
1996 - Pat Burrell, Miami (Fla.), 3b
1997 - Brandon Larson, LSU, ss
1998 - Wes Rachels, Southern Cal, 2b
1999 - Marshall McDougall, Fla. St., 2b
2000 - Trey Hodges, LSU, p
2001 - Charlton Jimerson, Miami (Fla.), of
2002 - Huston Street, Texas, p

The College World Series Record Book

Division I World Series Results

1947
Game 1 - California 17, Yale 4
Game 2 - California 8, Yale 7

1948
Game 1 - Southern Cal 3, Yale 1
Game 2 - Yale 8, So. Cal. 3
Game 3 - Southern Cal. 9, Yale 2

1949
Game 1 - Wake Forest 2, Southern Cal 1
Game 2 - Texas 7, St. John's 1
Game 3 - Texas 8, Wake Forest 1
Game 4 - So. Cal. 12, St. John's 4
Game 5 - Wake Forest 2, Southern Cal 1
Game 6 - Texas 10, Wake Forest 3

1950
Game 1 - Rutgers 4, Texas 2
Game 2 - Wisconsin 7, Colorado St. 3
Game 3 - Alabama 9, Bradley 2
Game 4 - Wash. St. 3, Tufts 1
Game 5 - Rutgers 5, Wisconsin 3
Game 6 - Wash. St. 9, Alabama 1
Game 7 - Texas 3, Colorado St. 1
Game 8 - Tufts 5, Bradley 4
Game 9 - Wash. St. 3, Rutgers 1
Game 10 - Texas 7, Tufts 0
Game 11 - Wisconsin 3, Alabama 1
Game 12 - Texas 12, Wash. St. 1
Game 13 - Rutgers 16, Wisconsin 2
Game 14 - Texas 15, Rutgers 9
Game 15 - Texas 3, Wash. St. 0

1951
Game 1 - So. Cal. 4, Princeton 1
Game 2 - Utah 7, Tennessee 1
Game 3 - Oklahoma 9, Ohio St. 8
Game 4 - Springfield 5, Texas A&M 1
Game 5 - Tennessee 3, Princeton 2
Game 6 - Texas A&M 3, Ohio St. 2
Game 7 - Southern Cal. 8, Utah 2
Game 8 - Oklahoma 7, Springfield 1
Game 9 - Tennessee 2, Springfield 0
Game 10 - Utah 15, Texas A&M 8
Game 11 - Oklahoma 4, Southern Cal. 1
Game 12 - Tennessee 5, Utah 4
Game 13 - Tennessee 9, So. Cal. 8
Game 14 - Oklahoma 3, Tennessee 2

1952
Game 1 - Penn St. 5, Texas 3
Game 2 - Duke 18, Oregon St. 7
Game 3 - Holy Cross 5, W. Mich. 1
Game 4 - Missouri 15, No. Colo. 1
Game 5 - Texas 10, Oregon St. 1
Game 6 - W. Mich. 8, No. Colo. 6
Game 7 - Penn St. 12, Duke 7
Game 8 - Missouri 1, Holy Cross 0
Game 9 - Holy Cross 2, Texas 1
Game 10 - W. Mich 5, Duke 1
Game 11 - Missouri 3, Penn St. 2
Game 12 - Holy Cross 15, W. Mich. 3
Game 13 - Holy Cross 15, Penn St. 4
Game 14 - Holy Cross 7, Missouri 3
Game 15 - Holy Cross 8, Missouri 4

1953
Game 1 - Lafayette 6, No. Colo. 2
Game 2 - Texas 2, Duke 1
Game 3 - Michigan 4, Stanford 0
Game 4 - Boston College 4, Houston 1
Game 5 - Duke 3, No. Colo. 2
Game 6 - Stanford 7, Houston 6
Game 7 - Texas 7, Lafayette 3
Game 8 - Michigan 6, Boston College 2
Game 9 - Boston College 7, Duke 6
Game 10 - Lafayette 4, Stanford 3
Game 11 - Michigan 12, Texas 5
Game 12 - Lafayette 2, Boston College 1
Game 13 - Texas 6, Michigan 4
Game 14 - Texas 13, Lafayette 3
Game 15 - Michigan 7, Texas 5

1954
Game 1 - Mich. St. 16, Mass. 5
Game 2 - Arizona 12, Oregon 1

Game 3 - Rollins 9, Okla. St. 5
Game 4 - Missouri 5, Lafayette 3
Game 5 - Mass. 5, Oregon 3
Game 6 - Okla. St. 4, Lafayette 2
Game 7 - Mich. St. 2, Arizona 1
Game 8 - Rollins 4, Missouri 1
Game 9 - Missouri 8, Mass. 1
Game 10 - Okla. St. 5, Arizona 4
Game 11 - Rollins 5, Mich. St. 4
Game 12 - Missouri 7, Okla. St. 3
Game 13 - Mich. St. 3, Rollins 2
Game 14 - Missouri 4, Mich. St. 3
Game 15 - Missouri 4, Rollins 1
1955
Game 1 - Wake Forest 1, Colgate 0
Game 2 - No. Colo. 2, Southern Cal 1
Game 3 - W. Mich. 4, Arizona 1
Game 4 - Okla. St. 5, Springfield 1
Game 5 - Colgate 6, Southern Cal 4
Game 6 - Arizona 6, Springfield 0
Game 7 - Wake Forest 10, No. Colo. 0
Game 8 - W. Mich. 5, Okla. St. 4
Game 9 - Okla. St. 4, Colgate 2
Game 10 - Arizona 20, No. Colo. 0
Game 11 - W. Mich. 9, Wake Forest 0
Game 12 - Okla. St. 5, Arizona 4
Game 13 - Wake Forest 10, W. Mich. 7
Game 14 - Wake Forest 2, Okla. St. 0
Game 15 - Wake Forest 7, W. Mich. 6
1956
Game 1 - Arizona 3, NYU 0
Game 2 - Minnesota 4, Wyoming 0
Game 3 - Miss. 13, New Hampshire 12
Game 4 - Bradley 4, Wash. St. 3
Game 5 - Wyoming 8, NYU 2
Game 6 - New Hampshire 6, Wash. St. 4
Game 7 - Minnesota 3, Arizona 1
Game 8 - Miss. 4, Bradley 0
Game 9 - Bradley 12, Wyoming 8
Game 10 - Arizona 1, New Hampshire 0
Game 11 - Minnesota 13, Miss. 5
Game 12 - Arizona 7, Miss. 3

Game 13 - Minnesota 8, Bradley 3
Game 14 - Arizona 10, Minnesota 4
Game 15 - Minnesota 12, Arizona 1
1957
Game 1 - Texas 3, Connecticut 0
Game 2 - Penn St. 7, Florida St. 0
Game 3 - California 4, No. Colo. 0
Game 4 - Iowa St. 13, Notre Dame 8
Game 5 - Connecticut 5, Florida St. 3
Game 6 - Notre Dame 23, No. Colo. 2
Game 7 - Penn St. 4, Texas 1
Game 8 - California 8, Iowa St. 2
Game 9 - Iowa St. 5, Connecticut 3
Game 10 - Notre Dame 9, Texas 0
Game 11 - California 8, Penn St. 0
Game 12 - Penn St. 5, Notre Dame 4
Game 13 - California 9, Iowa St. 1
Game 14 - California 1, Penn St. 0
1958
Game 1 - Missouri 3, W. Mich. 1
Game 2 - No. Colo. 10, Lafayette 5
Game 3 - Holy Cross 3, Southern Cal 0
Game 4 - Clemson 4, Arizona 1
Game 5 - W. Mich. 4, Lafayette 3
Game 6 - So. Cal. 4, Arizona 0
Game 7 - Missouri 11, No. Colo. 5
Game 8 - Holy Cross 17, Clemson 4
Game 9 - W. Mich. 5, Clemson 3
Game 10 - Southern Cal. 12, No. Colo. 1
Game 11 - Missouri 4, Holy Cross 1
Game 12 - So. Cal. 6, Holy Cross 2
Game 13 - Missouri 3, W. Mich. 1
Game 14 - Southern Cal 7, Missouri 0
Game 15 - Southern Cal 8, Missouri 7
1959
Game 1 - Okla. St. 10, W. Mich. 2
Game 2 - Penn St. 5, Connecticut 3
Game 3 - Arizona 3, Clemson 2
Game 4 - Fresno St. 6, No. Colo. 5
Game 5 - W. Mich. 14, Connecticut 6
Game 6 - Clemson 7, No. Colo. 1
Game 7 - Okla. St. 8, Penn St. 6

Game 8 - Arizona 5, Freso St. 1
Game 9 - Fresno St. 7, W. Mich. 2
Game 10 - Penn St. 7, Clemson 0
Game 11 - Arizona 5, Okla. St. 3
Game 12 - Okla. St. 4, Penn St. 3
Game 13 - Fresno St. 2, Arizona 0
Game 14 - Okla. St. 4, Fresno St. 0
Game 15 - Okla. St. 5, Arizona 3
1960
Game 1 - Arizona 2, Okla. St. 1
Game 2 - Minnesota 8, No. Carolina 3
Game 3 - Boston College 8, No. Colo. 3
Game 4 - So. Cal. 3, St. John's 1
Game 5 - Okla. St. 7, No. Carolina 0
Game 6 - St. John's 3, No. Colo. 2
Game 7 - Minnesota 8, Arizona 5
Game 8 - So. Cal. 5, Boston College 2
Game 9 - Okla. St. 1, Boston College 0
Game 10 - Arizona 11, St. John's 4
Game 11 - Minnesota 12, So. Cal. 11
Game 12 - So. Cal. 13, Arizona 1
Game 13 - Minnesota 3, Okla. St. 1
Game 14 - So. Cal. 4, Minnesota 3
Game 15 - Minnesota 2, So. Cal. 1
1961
Game 1 - Oklahoma St. 3, Duke 2
Game 2 - Syracuse 12, No. Colo. 5
Game 3 - Boston College 3, W. Mich. 2
Game 4 - So. Cal. 8, Texas 6
Game 5 - Duke 15, No. Colo. 3
Game 6 - W. Mich. 8, Texas 2
Game 7 - Okla. St. 12, Syracuse 9
Game 8 - So. Cal. 10, Boston College 3
Game 9 - Boston College 4, Duke 3
Game 10 - Syracuse 6, W. Mich. 0
Game 11 - So. Cal. 4, Okla. St. 2
Game 12 - Okla. St. 8, Syracuse 0
Game 13 - So. Cal. 4, Boston College 3
Game 14 - So. Cal. 1, Okla. St. 0
1962
Game 1 - Holy Cross 4, No. Colo. 3
Game 2 - Michigan 3, Texas 1

Game 3 - Ithaca 5, Missouri 1
Game 4 - Florida St. 6, Santa Clara 1
Game 5 - Texas 12, No. Colo. 2
Game 6 - Santa Clara 7, Missouri 4
Game 7 - Michigan 11, Holy Cross 4
Game 8 - Florida St. 5, Ithaca 4
Game 9 - Texas 3, Ithaca 2
Game 10 - Santa Clara 12, Holy Cross 7
Game 11 - Michigan 10, Florida St. 7
Game 12 - Santa Clara 11, Florida St. 6
Game 13 - Texas 7, Michigan 0
Game 14 - Santa Clara 4, Texas 3
Game 15 - Michigan 5, Santa Clara 4
1963
Game 1 - Arizona 8, Penn St. 1
Game 2 - Florida St. 5, W. Mich. 2
Game 3 - Texas 8, So. Cal. 3
Game 4 - Missouri 3, Holy Cross 0
Game 5 - Penn St. 3, W. Mich. 0
Game 6 - So. Cal., 6, Holy Cross 5
Game 7 - Arizona 4, Florida St. 3
Game 8 - Missouri 3, Texas 2
Game 9 - Texas 6, Penn St. 4
Game 10 - So. Cal. 4, Florida St. 3
Game 11 - Arizona 6, Missouri 4
Game 12 - So. Cal. 12, Missouri 3
Game 13 - Arizona 10, Texas 8
Game 14 - So. Cal. 6, Arizona 4
Game 15 - So. Cal. 5, Arizona 2
1964
Game 1 - Maine 5, Seton Hall 1
Game 2 - Minnesota 7, Texas A&M 3
Game 3 - So. Cal. 3, Mississippi 2
Game 4 - Missouri 7, Arizona St. 0
Game 5 - Seton Hall 14, Texas A&M 5
Game 6 - Arizona St. 5, Mississippi 0
Game 7 - Minnesota 12, Maine 0
Game 8 - So. Cal. 3, Missouri 2
Game 9 - Missouri 3, Seton Hall 1
Game 10 - Maine 4, Arizona St. 2
Game 11 - Minnesota 6, So. Cal. 5
Game 12 - Maine 2, So. Cal. 1

The College World Series Record Book

Game 13 - Missouri 4, Minnesota 1
Game 14 - Missouri 2, Maine 1
Game 15 - Minnesota 5, Missouri 1
1965
Game 1 - Ohio St. 2, Florida St. 1
Game 2 - Wash. St. 12, Texas 5
Game 3 - Arizona St. 14, Lafayette 1
Game 4 - St. Louis 2, Connecticut 1
Game 5 - Florida St. 3, Texas 2
Game 6 - Connecticut 6, Lafayette 4
Game 7 - Ohio St. 14, Wash. St. 1
Game 8 - Arizona St. 13, St. Louis 3
Game 9 - St. Louis 5, Florida St. 3
Game 10 - Wash. St. 3, Connecticut 2
Game 11 - Arizona St. 9, Ohio St. 4
Game 12 - Ohio St. 1, Wash. St. 0
Game 13 - Arizona St. 6, St. Louis 2
Game 14 - Ohio St. 7, Arizona St. 3
Game 15 - Arizona St. 2, Ohio St. 1
1966
Game 1 - Texas 5, Arizona 1
Game 2 - St. John's 5, Northeastern 3
Game 3 - So. Cal. 6, No. Carolina 2
Game 4 - Ohio St. 4, Okla. St. 2
Game 5 - Arizona 8, Northeastern 1
Game 6 - Okla. St. 5, No. Carolina 1
Game 7 - St. John's 2, Texas 0
Game 8 - Ohio St. 6, So. Cal. 2
Game 9 - So. Cal. 8, Arizona 4
Game 10 - Okla. St. 6, Texas 1
Game 11 - Ohio St. 8, St. John's 7
Game 12 - Okla. St. 6, St. John's 1
Game 13 - So. Cal. 5, Ohio St. 1
Game 14 - Ohio St. 1, So. Cal. 0
Game 15 - Ohio St. 8, Okla. St. 2
1967
Game 1 - Stanford 12, Houston 1
Game 2 - Auburn 1, Ohio St. 0
Game 3 - Boston College 3, Rider 1
Game 4 - Arizona St. 7, Okla. St. 2
Game 5 - Houston 7, Ohio St. 6
Game 6 - Rider 3, Okla. St. 1

Game 7 - Stanford 6, Auburn 3
Game 8 - Arizona St. 8, Stanford 1
Game 9 - Houston 3, Boston College 2
Game 10 - Auburn 4, Rider 3
Game 11 - Arizona St. 5, Stanford 3
Game 12 - Stanford 5, Auburn 3
Game 13 - Houston 3, Arizona St. 0
Game 14 - Arizona St. 4, Stanford 3
Game 15 - Arizona St 11, Houston 2
1968
Game 1 - St. John's 2, Harvard 0
Game 2 - No. Carolina 7, So. Ill. 6
Game 3 - So. Ill. 2, Harvard 1
Game 4 - Okla. St. 8, Texas 5
Game 5 - So. Cal. 5, Brigham Young 3
Game 6 - Texas 7, Brigham Young 0
Game 7 - St. John's 3, No. Carolina 2
Game 8 - So. Cal. 6, Okla. St. 5
Game 9 - No. Carolina 6, Texas 5
Game 10 - So. Ill. 7, Okla. St. 1
Game 11 - So. Cal. 7, St. John's 6
Game 12 - So. Ill 15, St. John's 0
Game 13 - So. Cal. 2, No. Carolina 0
Game 14 - So. Cal. 4, So. Ill. 3
1969
Game 1 - Texas 4, Arizona St. 0
Game 2 - Tulsa 6, UCLA 5
Game 3 - Arizona St. 2, UCLA 1
Game 4 - Massachusetts 2, So. Ill. 0
Game 5 - NYU 8, Mississippi 3
Game 6 - Mississippi 8, So. Ill. 1
Game 7 - Tulsa 4, Texas 2
Game 8 - NYU 9, Massachusetts 2
Game 9 - Texas 14, Mississippi 1
Game 10 - Arizona St. 4, Mass. 2
Game 11 - Tulsa 2, NYU 0
Game 12 - NYU 3, Texas 2
Game 13 - Arizona St. 11, Tulsa 3
Game 14 - Arizona St. 4, NYU 1
Game 15 - Arizona St. 10, Tulsa 1
1970
Game 1 - Texas 12, Delaware 4

Game 2 - Ohio 4, Southern Cal 1
Game 3 - Southern Cal 7, Delaware 1
Game 4 - Florida St. 4, Arizona 0
Game 5 - Dartmouth 7, Iowa St. 6
Game 6 - Iowa St. 7, Arizona 1
Game 7 - Texas 7, Ohio 2
Game 8 - Florida St. 6, Dartmouth 0
Game 9 - Ohio 9, Iowa St. 6
Game 10 - Southern Cal 6, Dartmouth 1
Game 11 - Texas 5, Florida St. 1
Game 12 - Florida St. 2, Ohio 0
Game 13 - Southern Cal 8, Texas 7
Game 14 - Florida St. 11, Texas 2
Game 15 - Southern Cal 2, Florida St. 1

1971

Game 1 - BYU 4, Harvard 1
Game 2 - Tulsa 5, Mississippi St. 2
Game 3 - BYU 3, Mississippi St. 1
Game 4 - Southern Cal 5, Seton Hall 1
Game 5 - So. Illinois 5, Tex.-Pan Am. 4
Game 6 - Tex.-Pan Am. 8, Seton Hall 2
Game 7 - Tulsa 9, Harvard 8
Game 8 - So. Ill. 8, Southern Cal 3
Game 9 - Tex.-Pan Am. 1, Harvard 0
Game 10 - Southern Cal 8, BYU 6
Game 11 - Tulsa 9, So. Illinois 4
Game 12 - So. Ill. 8, Tex.-Pan Am. 6
Game 13 - So. Cal. 8, Tulsa 4
Game 14 - So. Cal. 3, Tulsa 2
Game 15 - So. Cal. 7, So. Ill. 2

1972

Game 1 - Southern Cal 8, Mississippi 6
Game 2 - Connecticut 3, Texas 0
Game 3 - Texas 9, Mississippi 8
Game 4 - Oklahoma 2, Temple 1
Game 5 - Arizona St. 2, Iowa 1
Game 6 - Temple 13, Iowa 9
Game 7 - Southern Cal 5, Connecticut 4
Game 8 - Arizona St. 1, Oklahoma 0
Game 9 - Temple 7, Connecticut 4
Game 10 - Texas 7, Oklahoma 1
Game 11 - Arizona St. 3, Southern Cal 0

Game 12 - Southern Cal 4, Texas 3
Game 13 - Arizona St. 1, Temple 0
Game 14 - Southern Cal 3, Arizona St. 1
Game 15 - Southern Cal 1, Arizona St. 0

1973

Game 1 - Minnesota 1, Oklahoma 0
Game 2 - Arizona St. 3, Penn St. 1
Game 3 - Oklahoma 6, Penn St. 0
Game 4 - Texas 6, Ga. Southern 3
Game 5 - So. Cal. 4, Harvard 1
Game 6 - Ga. Southern 8, Harvard 0
Game 7 - Arizona St. 3, Minnesota 0
Game 8 - Southern Cal. 4, Texas 1
Game 9 - Minnesota 6, Ga. Southern 2
Game 10 - Texas 10, Oklahoma 2
Game 11 - So. Cal. 3, Arizona St. 1
Game 12 - Arizona St. 6, Texas 5
Game 13 - So. Cal 8, Minnesota 7
Game 14 - So. Cal. 4, Arizona St. 3

1974

Game 1 - Miami 4, Harvard 1
Game 2 - Oklahoma 10, No. Colo. 1
Game 3 - No. Colo. 4, Harvard 2
Game 4 - So. Cal 9, Texas 2
Game 5 - So. Ill. 5, Seton Hall 1
Game 6 - Texas 12, Seton Hall 2
Game 7 - Miami 5, Oklahoma 1
Game 8 - So. Cal. 5, So. Ill. 3
Game 9 - Texas 10, Oklahoma 4
Game 10 - So. Ill. 5, No. Colo. 3
Game 11 - Miami 7, So. Cal. 3
Game 12 - So. Cal. 5, Texas 3
Game 13 - So. Ill. 4, Miami 3
Game 14 - So. Cal. 7, So. Ill. 2
Game 15 - So. Cal. 7, Miami 3

1975

Game 1 - Arizona St. 5, Cal St. Ful. 3
Game 2 - Texas 4, Oklahoma 2
Game 3 - Oklahoma 11, Cal St. Ful. 4
Game 4 - South Carolina 3, Seton Hall 1
Game 5 - E. Mich. 2, Florida St. 1
Game 6 - Seton Hall 11, Florida St. 0

Game 7 - Arizona St. 5, Cal St. Ful. 2
Game 8 - So. Carolina 5, E. Mich. 1
Game 9 - Texas 12, Seton Hall 10
Game 10 - Oklahoma 7, E. Mich. 0
Game 11 - So. Carolina 6, Arizona St. 3
Game 12 - Arizona St. 1, Oklahoma 0
Game 13 - Texas 17, South Carolina 6
Game 14 - So. Carolina 4, Arizona St. 1
Game 15 - Texas 5, So. Carolina 1
1976
Game 1 - Clemson 9, Auburn 4
Game 2 - E. Mich. 3, Maine 2
Game 3 - Maine 9, Auburn 8
Game 4 - Arizona St. 7, Arizona 6
Game 5 - Washington St. 6, Oklahoma 1
Game 6 - Arizona 10, Oklahoma 2
Game 7 - E. Mich. 3, Clemson 2
Game 8 - Arizona St. 9, Wash. St. 3
Game 9 - Arizona 10, Clemson 6
Game 10 - Maine 6, Washington St. 3
Game 11 - E. Mich. 2, Arizona St. 1
Game 12 - Arizona St. 7, Maine 0
Game 13 - Arizona 11, E. Mich. 6
Game 14 - Arizona 5, Arizona St. 1
Game 15 - Arizona 7, East. Mich. 1
1977
Game 1 - So. Ill. 10, Temple 5
Game 2 - Arizona St. 10, Clemson 7
Game 3 - Clemson 13, Temple 4
Game 4 - Cal St. LA 7, Minnesota 4
Game 5 - So. Carolina 3, Baylor 2
Game 6 - Minnesota 4, Arizona St. 3
Game 7 - So. Ill. 3, Arizona St. 2
Game 8 - So. Carolina 6, Cal St. LA 2
Game 9 - Arizona St. 8, Minnesota 4
Game 10 - Cal St. LA 1, Clemson 0
Game 11 - So. Carolina 5, So. Ill 4
Game 12 - So. Ill. 9, Cal St. LA 7
Game 13 - Arizona St. 6, So. Carolina 2
Game 14 - Arizona St. 10, So. Ill. 0
Game 15 - Arizona St. 2, So. Carolina 1
1978

Game 1 - Michigan 4, Baylor 0
Game 2 - Southern Cal 9, Miami (Fla.) 3
Game 3 - Miami (Fla.) 12, Baylor 1
Game 4 - Oral Roberts 11, N. Carolina 0
Game 5 - Arizona State 13, St. John's 2
Game 6 - N. Carolina 9, St. John's 5
Game 7 - So. Cal 11, Michigan 3
Game 8 - Arizona St. 7, Oral Roberts 6
Game 9 - No. Carolina 7, Michigan 6
Game 10 - Miami (Fla.) 5, Oral Roberts 3
Game 11 - Southern Cal 5, Arizona St. 2
Game 12 - Arizona St. 11, Miami (Fla.) 3
Game 13 - Southern Cal 3, N. Carolina 2
Game 14 - Southern Cal 10, Arizona St. 3
1979
Game 1 - Arkansas 5, Pepperdine 4
Game 2 - Arizona 5, Miami (Fla.) 1
Game 3 - Pepperdine 9, Miami (Fla.) 3
Game 4 - Texas 11, Conn. 5
Game 5 - Miss. St. 6, Cal St. Ful. 1
Game 6 - Cal St. Ful. 8, Conn. 3
Game 7 - Arkansas 10, Arizona 3
Game 8 - Texas 8, Miss. St. 2
Game 9 - Cal St. Ful. 16, Arizona 3
Game 10 - Pepperdine 5, Miss. St. 4
Game 11 - Arkansas 9, Texas 4
Game 12 - Pepperdine 6, Texas 4
Game 13 - Cal St. Ful. 13, Arkansas 10
Game 14 - Cal St. Ful. 8, Pepperdine 5
Game 15 - Cal St. Ful. 2, Arkansas 1
1980
Game 1 - St. John's 6, Arizona 1
Game 2 - Hawaii 7, Florida St. 6
Game 3 - Arizona 5, Florida St. 3
Game 4 - Miami (Fla.) 13, Clemson 5
Game 5 - Michigan 9, California 8
Game 6 - California 6, Clemson 4
Game 7 - Hawaii 7, St. John's 2
Game 8 - Miami (Fla.) 3, Michigan 2
Game 9 - California 8, St. John's 5
Game 10 - Arizona 8, Michigan 0
Game 11 - Hawaii 9, Miami (Fla.) 3

Game 12 - California 4, Miami (Fla.) 3
Game 13 - Arizona 6, Hawaii 4
Game 14 - Arizona 11, California 10
Game 15 - Arizona 5, Hawaii 3

1981
Game 1 - Mississippi St. 4, Michigan 0
Game 2 - Arizona St. 11, Texas 2
Game 3 - Oklahoma St. 8, So. Carolina 5
Game 4 - Miami (Fla.) 6, Maine 1
Game 5 - Texas 6, Michigan 5
Game 6 - So. Carolina 12, Maine 7
Game 7 - Arizona St. 4, Mississippi St. 3
Game 8 - Oklahoma St. 12, Miami (Fla.) 6
Game 9 - So. Carolina 6, Mississippi St. 5
Game 10 - Texas 5, Miami (Fla.) 4
Game 11 - Okla. St. 11, Arizona St. 10
Game 12 - Arizona St. 10, S. Carolina 7
Game 13 - Texas 15, Oklahoma St. 8
Game 14 - Arizona St. 12, Texas 3
Game 15 - Arizona St. 7, Oklahoma St. 4

1982
Game 1 - Miami (Fla.) 7, Maine 2
Game 2 - Wichita St. 7, Cal St. Ful. 0
Game 3 - Texas 9, Oklahoma St. 1
Game 4 - Stanford 15, S. Carolina 4
Game 5 - Maine 6, Cal St. Ful. 0
Game 6 - Oklahoma St. 10, S. Carolina 8
Game 7 - Miami (Fla.) 4, Wichita St. 3
Game 8 - Texas 8, Stanford 6
Game 9 - Wichita St. 13, Oklahoma St. 2
Game 10 - Maine 8, Stanford 5
Game 11 - Miami (Fla.) 2, Texas 1
Game 12 - Wichita St. 8, Texas 4
Game 13 - Miami (Fla.) 10, Maine 4
Game 14 - Miami (Fla.) 9, Wichita St. 3

1983
Game 1 - Texas 12, James Madison 0
Game 2 - Oklahoma St. 3, Stanford 1
Game 3 - Michigan 6, Maine 5
Game 4 - Alabama 6, Arizona St. 5
Game 5 - Stanford 3, James Madison 1
Game 6 - Arizona St. 7, Maine 0

Game 7 - Texas 6, Oklahoma St. 5
Game 8 - Alabama 6, Michigan 5
Game 9 - Arizona St. 6, Oklahoma St. 5
Game 10 - Michigan 11, Stanford 4
Game 11 - Texas 6, Alabama 4
Game 12 - Alabama 6, Arizona St. 0
Game 13 - Texas 4, Michigan 2
Game 14 - Texas 4, Alabama 3

1984
Game 1 - Texas 6, New Orleans 3
Game 2 - Cal St. Ful. 8, Michigan 4
Game 3 - Arizona St. 9, Miami (Fla.) 6
Game 4 - Oklahoma St. 9, Maine 5
Game 5 - New Orleans 11, Michigan 3
Game 6 - Maine 13, Miami 7
Game 7 - Texas 6, Cal St. Ful. 4
Game 8 - Arizona St. 23, Oklahoma St. 12
Game 9 - Cal St. Ful. 13, Miami (Fla.) 5
Game 10 - Oklahoma St 8, New Orleans 7
Game 11 - Texas 8, Arizona St. 4
Game 12 - Cal St. Ful. 6, Arizona St. 1
Game 13 - Oklahoma St. 18, Texas 13
Game 14 - Cal St. Ful. 10, Oklahoma St. 2
Game 15 - Cal St. Ful. 3, Texas 1

1985
Game 1 - Arkansas 1, So. Carolina 0
Game 2 - Miss. St. 12, Oklahoma St. 3
Game 3 - Miami (Fla.) 17, Stanford 3
Game 4 - Texas 2, Arizona 1
Game 5 - Okla. St. 16, So. Carolina 11
Game 6 - Stanford 9, Arizona 2
Game 7 - Mississippi St. 5, Arkansas 4
Game 8 - Texas 8, Miami (Fla.) 4
Game 9 - Arkansas 10, Stanford 9
Game 10 - Miami (Fla.) 2, Okla. St. 1
Game 11 - Texas 12, Miss. St. 7
Game 12 - Miami (Fla.) 6, Miss. St. 5
Game 13 - Texas 8, Arkansas 7
Game 14 - Miami (Fla.) 2, Texas 1
Game 15 - Miami (Fla.) 10, Texas 6

1986
Game 1 - Loyola Marymount 4, LSU 3

Game 2 - Arizona 8, Maine 7
Game 3 - Miami (Fla.) 6, Oklahoma St. 2
Game 4 - Florida St. 5, Indiana St. 3
Game 5 - LSU 8, Maine 4
Game 6 - Oklahoma St. 4, Indiana St. 0
Game 7 - Arizona 7, Loyola Marymount 5
Game 8 - Florida St. 7, Miami (Fla.) 2
Game 9 - Ok. St. 11, Loyola Marymount 5
Game 10 - Miami (Fla.) 4, LSU 3
Game 11 - Arizona 9, Florida St. 5
Game 12 - Florida St. 6, Okla. St. 5
Game 13 - Miami (Fla.) 4, Arizona 2
Game 14 - Florida St. 4, Miami (Fla.) 3
Game 15 - Arizona 10, Florida St. 2
1987
Game 1 - Oklahoma St. 8, Arizona St. 3
Game 2 - LSU 6, Florida St. 2
Game 3 - Texas 13, Arkansas 6
Game 4 - Stanford 3, Georgia 2
Game 5 - Florida St. 3, Arizona St. 0
Game 6 - Arkansas 5, Georgia 4
Game 7 - Oklahoma St. 8, LSU 7
Game 8 - Stanford 6, Texas 1
Game 9 - LSU 5, Arkansas 2
Game 10 - Texas 6, Florida St. 4
Game 11 - Oklahoma St. 6, Stanford 2
Game 12 - Stanford 6, LSU 5
Game 13 - Texas 6, Oklahoma St. 5
Game 14 - Stanford 9, Texas 3
Game 15 - Stanford 9, Oklahoma St. 5
1988
Game 1 - Arizona St. 4, California 2
Game 2 - Wichita St. 5, Florida 4
Game 3 - Stanford 10, Fresno St. 3
Game 4 - Cal St. Ful. 9, Miami (Fla.) 3
Game 5 - Florida 6, California 5
Game 6 - Wichita St. 7, Arizona St. 4
Game 7 - Miami (Fla.) 8, Fresno St. 4
Game 8 - Cal St. Ful. 5, Stanford 3
Game 9 - Arizona St. 10, Florida 1
Game 10 - Stanford 2, Miami (Fla.) 1
Game 11 - Arizona St. 4, Wichita St. 3

Game 12 - Stanford 4, Cal St. Ful. 1
Game 13 - Arizona St. 19, Wichita St. 1
Game 14 - Stanford 9, Cal St. Ful. 5
Game 15 - Stanford 9, Arizona St. 4
1989
Game 1 - Florida St. 4, No. Carolina 2
Game 2 - Wichita St. 3, Arkansas 1
Game 3 - Texas 7, Long Beach St. 1
Game 4 - Miami (Fla.) 5, LSU 2
Game 5 - Arkansas 7, No. Carolina 3
Game 6 - Florida St. 4, Wichita St. 2
Game 7 - LSU 8, Long Beach St. 5
Game 8 - Texas 12, Miami (Fla.) 2
Game 9 - Wichita St. 8, Arkansas 4
Game 10 - LSU 6, Miami (Fla.) 3
Game 11 - Wichita St. 7, Florida St. 4
Game 12 - Texas 12, LSU 7
Game 13 - Wichita St. 12, Florida St. 9
Game 14 - Wichita St. 5, Texas 3
1990
Game 1 - Stanford 5, Ga. Southern 4
Game 2 - Georgia 3, Miss. St. 0
Game 3 - LSU 8, Citadel 2
Game 4 - Okla. St. 14, Cal. St. Ful. 4
Game 5 - Miss. St. 15, Ga. Southern 1
Game 6 - Georgia 16, Stanford 2
Game 7 - Citadel 8, Cal St. Ful. 7
Game 8 - Oklahoma St. 7, LSU 1
Game 9 - Stanford 6, Miss. St. 1
Game 10 - LSU 6, Citadel 1
Game 11 - Stanford 4, Georgia 2
Game 12 - Oklahoma St. 14, LSU 3
Game 13 - Georgia 5, Stanford 1
Game 14 - Georgia 2, Oklahoma St. 1
1991
Game 1 - Fresno St. 6, Florida St. 3
Game 2 - LSU 8, Florida 1
Game 3 - Creighton 8, Clemson 4
Game 4 - Wichita St. 8, Long Beach St. 5
Game 5 - Florida 5, Florida St. 0
Game 6 - LSU 15, Fresno St. 3
Game 7 - Long Beach St 12, Clemson 11

15

Game 8 - Wichita St. 3, Creighton 2
Game 9 - Florida 2, Fresno St. 1
Game 10 - Creighton 13, Long Beach St. 4
Game 11 - LSU 19, Florida 8
Game 12 - Wichita St. 11, Creighton 3
Game 13 - LSU 5, Wichita St. 3
1992
Game 1 - Miami (Fla.) 4, California 3
Game 2 - Cal St. Ful. 7, Florida St. 2
Game 3 - Pepperdine 6, Wichita St. 0
Game 4 - Texas 15, Oklahoma 3
Game 5 - Florida St. 5, California 4
Game 6 - Miami (Fla.) 4, Cal St. Ful. 3
Game 7 - Oklahoma 8, Wichita St. 4
Game 8 - Pepperdine 7, Texas 0
Game 9 - Cal St. Ful. 6, Florida St. 0
Game 10 - Texas 8, Oklahoma 5
Game 11 - Cal St. Ful. 7, Miami (Fla.) 5
Game 12 - Pepperdine 5, Texas 4
Game 13 - Cal St. Ful. 8, Miami 1
Game 14 - Pepperdine 3, Cal St. Ful. 2
1993
Game 1 - Texas A&M 5, Kansas 1
Game 2 - LSU 7, Long Beach St. 1
Game 3 - Wichita St. 4, Arizona St. 3
Game 4 - Texas 6, Oklahoma St. 5
Game 5 - Long Beach St. 6, Kansas 1
Game 6 - LSU 13, Texas A&M 8
Game 7 - Oklahoma St. 5, Arizona St. 4
Game 8 - Wichita St. 7, Texas 6
Game 9 - Long Beach St. 6, Tex. A&M 2
Game 10 - Oklahoma St. 7, Texas 6
Game 11 - Long Beach St. 10, LSU 8
Game 12 - Wichita St. 10, Oklahoma St. 4
Game 13 - LSU 6, Long Beach St. 5
Game 14 - LSU 8, Wichita St. 0
1994
Game 1 - Georgia Tech 2, Cal St. Ful. 0
Game 2 - Florida St. 6, LSU 3
Game 3 - Arizona St. 4, Miami (Fla.) 0
Game 4 - Oklahoma 5, Auburn 4
Game 5 - Georgia Tech 12, Florida St. 4

Game 6 - Cal. St. Ful. 20, LSU 6
Game 7 - Miami (Fla.) 7, Auburn 5
Game 8 - Oklahoma 4, Arizona St. 3
Game 9 - Cal St. Ful. 10, Florida St. 3
Game 10 - Arizona St. 9, Miami (Fla.) 5
Game 11 - Georgia Tech 3, Cal St. Ful. 2
Game 12 - Oklahoma 6, Arizona St. 1
Game 13 - Oklahoma 13, Georgia Tech 5
1995
Game 1 - Florida St. 3, Oklahoma 2
Game 2 - Miami (Fla.) 15, So. Cal. 10
Game 3 - Cal St. Ful. 6, Stanford 5
Game 4 - Tennessee 3, Clemson 1
Game 5 - Miami (Fla.) 4, Florida St. 2
Game 6 - Southern Cal 9, Oklahoma 4
Game 7 - Cal St. Ful. 11, Tennessee 1
Game 8 - Stanford 8, Clemson 3
Game 9 - Southern Cal 16, Florida St 11
Game 10 - Tennessee 6, Stanford 2
Game 11 - Southern Cal 7, Miami (Fla.) 5
Game 12 - Cal. St. Ful. 11, Tennessee 0
Game 13 - So. Cal. 7, Miami (Fla.) 3
Game 14 - Cal St. Ful. 11, Southern Cal 5
1996
Game 1 - Alabama 7, Oklahoma St. 5
Game 2 - Miami (Fla.) 7, Clemson 3
Game 3 - Florida 5, Florida St. 2
Game 4 - LSU 9, Wichita St. 8
Game 5 - Miami (Fla.) 15, Alabama 1
Game 6 - Clemson 8, Oklahoma St. 5
Game 7 - LSU 9, Florida 4
Game 8 - Florida St. 8, Wichita St. 4
Game 9 - Clemson 14, Alabama 13
Game 10 - Florida 6, Florida St. 3
Game 11 - Miami (Fla.) 14, Clemson 5
Game 12 - LSU 2, Florida 1
Game 13 - LSU 9, Miami (Fla.) 8
1997
Game 1 - Stanford 8, Auburn 3
Game 2 - LSU 5, Rice 4
Game 3 - Miami (Fla.) 7, UCLA 3
Game 4 - Alabama 3, Miss. St. 2

Game 5 - LSU 10, Stanford 5
Game 6 - Auburn 10, Rice 1
Game 7 - Miami (Fla.) 6, Alabama 1
Game 8 - Miss. St. 7, UCLA 5
Game 9 - Stanford 11, Auburn 4
Game 10 - Alabama 9, Miss. St. 5
Game 11 - LSU 13, Stanford 9
Game 12 - Alabama 8, Miami (Fla.) 6
Game 13 - Alabama 8, Miami (Fla.) 2
Game 14 - LSU 13, Alabama 6
1998
Game 1 - Arizona St. 11, Florida St. 10
Game 2 - Miami (Fla.) 3, Long Beach St. 1
Game 3 - LSU 12, Southern Cal 10
Game 4 - Miss. St. 14, Florida 13
Game 5 - Arizona St. 9, Miami (Fla.) 2
Game 6 - Long Beach St. 7, Florida 4
Game 7 - LSU 10, Miss. St. 8
Game 8 - Southern Cal 12, Florida 10
Game 9 - Long Beach St. 6, Miami 3
Game 10 - Southern Cal 7, Miss. St. 1
Game 11 - Arizona St. 14, Long Beach 4
Game 12 - Southern Cal 5, LSU 4
Game 13 - Southern Cal 7, LSU 3
Game 14 - So. Cal 21, Arizona St. 14
1999
Game 1 - Alabama 11, Oklahoma St. 3
Game 2 - Miami (Fla.) 8, Rice 4
Game 3 - Florida St. 7, Texas A&M 3
Game 4 - Stanford 9, Cal. St. Ful. 2
Game 5 - Miami (Fla.) 8, Alabama 1
Game 6 - Rice 7, Oklahoma St. 2
Game 7 - Stanford 10, Florida St. 6
Game 8 - Cal St. Ful. 4, Texas A&M 2
Game 9 - Alabama 6, Rice 5
Game 10 - Florida St. 7, Cal. St. Ful. 2
Game 11 - Miami (Fla.) 5, Alabama 2
Game 12 - Florida St. 8, Stanford 6
Game 13 - Florida St. 14, Stanford 11
Game 14 - Miami (Fla.) 6, Florida St. 5
2000
Game 1 - Clemson 10, San Jose St. 6

The College World Series Record Book

Game 2 - Stanford 6, La.-Lafayette 4
Game 3 - Southern Cal 6, Florida St. 4
Game 4 - LSU 13, Texas 5
Game 5 - Stanford 10, Clemson 4
Game 6 - La.-Lafayette 6, San Jose St. 3
Game 7 - LSU 10, Southern Cal 4
Game 8 - Florida St. 6, Texas 2
Game 9 - La-Lafayette 5, Clemson 4
Game 10 - Florida St. 3, Southern Cal 2
Game 11 - Stanford 19, La-Lafayette 9
Game 12 - LSU 6, Florida St. 3
Game 13 - LSU 6, Stanford 5
2001
Game 1 - Stanford 13, Tulane 11
Game 2 - Cal St. Ful. 5, Nebraska 4
Game 3 - Southern Cal 11, Georgia 5
Game 4 - Miami (Fla.) 21, Tennessee 13
Game 5 - Tulane 6, Nebraska 5
Game 6 - Stanford 5, Cal. St. Ful. 2
Game 7 - Tennessee 19, Georgia 12
Game 8 - Miami (Fla.) 4, Southern Cal 3
Game 9 - Cal St. Ful. 11, Tulane 2
Game 10 - Tennessee 10, Southern Cal 2
Game 11 - Stanford 4, Cal St. Ful. 1
Game 12 - Miami (Fla.) 12, Tennessee 6
Game 13 - Miami (Fla.) 12, Stanford 1
2002
Game 1 - Georgia Tech 11, So. Carolina 0
Game 2 - Clemson 11, Nebraska 10
Game 3 - Stanford 4, Notre Dame 3
Game 4 - Texas 2, Rice 1
Game 5 - So. Carolina 10, Nebraska 8
Game 6 - Clemson 9, Georgia Tech 7
Game 7 - Notre Dame 5, Rice 3
Game 8 - Texas 8, Stanford 7
Game 9 - So. Carolina 9, Georgia Tech 5
Game 10 - Stanford 5, Notre Dame 3
Game 11 - So. Carolina 12, Clemson 4
Game 12 - Texas 6, Stanford 5
Game 13 - S. Carolina 10, Clemson 2
Game 14 - Texas 12, So. Carolina 6

The College World Series Record Book

Boxscores from National Championship Finals
1947

First game, June 27, 1947

Yale	ab	r	h	California	ab	r	h
Davis, 2b	3	1	1	Palmer, cf	5	3	3
Elwell, lf	4	1	0	McClain, rf	5	1	1
Moher, ss	3	1	1	Brown, ss	5	2	2
Matthews, 3b	3	0	1	Fascalini, lf	3	3	1
Howe, rf	2	0	1	SanClemente, 3b	5	2	2
Felske, c	4	0	0	O'Dell, 1st	4	1	1
Bush, 1b	4	0	0	Ramos, 2b	4	1	1
Rosenweig, cf	3	1	1	Clayton, c	2	0	0
Quinn, p	2	0	0	Melton, c	0	2	0
Rossner, p	0	0	0	Barnise, p	0	0	0
Kemp, p	0	0	0	Larner, p	5	2	2
Bracnara, ph	1	0	0	Jensen, p	1	0	1
Totals	19	4	5	Totals	39	17	14

California   200 000 22 11 - 17
Yale   210 000 000 - 4

2B - Mathews. 3B - Brown. DP - Moher-Bush. S - Moher, Howe, McClain. BB - Quinn, 2, Rossner, 1, Kemp 2, Barnise, 2, Larner, 4. SO - Quinn 0, Kemp 1, Larner 3. WP - Kemp. SB - Davis, Mathews, SanClemente, O'Dell. Umpires - Edwin Hurley and William McKinley. HBP - Quinn (Fiscaline), Rosner (Melton). W - Larner. L - Quinn. A - 2,000. T - 2:23.

Lead-off hitter Lyle Palmer helped California to the first College World Series title in 1947.

Second Game, June 28, 1947

Yale	ab	r	h	California	ab	r	h
Davis, 2b	4	2	1	Palmer, cf	2	1	2
Elwell, lf	4	1	2	McClain, rf	5	1	1
Moher, ss	4	1	1	Brown, ss	4	0	0
Mathews, 3b	4	1	2	Cronin, ss	1	0	0
Howe, rf	5	1	2	Fiscalini, lf	5	3	4
Felske, c	5	0	1	SanClemente, 3b	5	2	2
Bush, 1b	3	1	0	O'Dell, 1b	4	0	1
Rosenweig, cf	2	0	1	Jensen, p	1	0	0
Sulliman, cf	2	0	1	Ramos, 2b	4	1	2
Duffus, p	0	0	0	Butler, p	1	0	0
Goodyear, p	2	0	0	Clayton, c	2	0	0
Totals	35	7	10	Totals	34	8	13

Yale   111 004 100 - 7
California   202 210 10x - 8

2B - Davis. 3B - Howe. SO - Jensen 4, Butler 2, Duffus 1, Goodyear 1. BB - Jensen 6, Butler 1. WP - Butler. S - Clayton, Duffus. SB - Davis, Bush, Palmer, Fiscaline, McClain. PB - Clayton 1. U - McKinley, Hurley. W - McKinley, Hurley.

1948

First Game, June 25, 1948

Southern California	ab	r	h	Yale	ab	r	h
Jones, cf	5	0	1	Moher, ss	3	0	0
Mazmanian, 2b	4	0	1	Goodyear, rf	4	0	0
Brideweser, ss	3	0	0	Redden, cf	3	0	0

Abbreviations

A - attendance
ab - at-bats
BB - base on balls
BK - balk
DP - double plays
E - errors
h - hits
HBP - hit by pitch
HR - home run
HO - hits off
IP - innings pitched
L - losing pitcher
LOB - left on base
PB - passed ball
R - runs
RBI - runs batted in
S - sacrifice
SB - stolen base
SF - sacrifice fly
SO - strikeouts
SV - save
T - time
U - umpires
W - winning pitcher
WP - wild pitch
2B - two-base hit
3B - three-base hit

The College World Series Record Book

	ab	r	h		ab	r	h
Workman, lf	4	0	0	Rosenweig, cf	1	0	1
McKelvey, c	4	0	2	Mathews, 3b	3	0	0
Zuber, c	0	0	0	Fitzgerald, lf	4	0	2
Henley, rf	4	0	1	Felske, c	3	0	1
Lillie, 3b	4	1	1	Russ, c	0	0	0
Cecillos, 1b	4	1	2	Bush, 1b	3	1	0
Hood, p	3	0	1	Smith, 2b	3	0	0
Freeman, ph	0	1	0	Duffus, p	2	0	0
				Breen, ph	1	0	0
Totals	35	3	9	Totals	29	1	4

Southern California 000 000 003- 3
Yale 001 000 000- 1

2B - Fitzgerald. S - Mazmanian. SB - Brideweser, Henley. DP - Moher-Smith-Bush. TP - Hood-Zuber-Cecillos-Lillie. SO - by Hood, 6, by Duffus, 3. BB - Hood 3, Duffus 2. LOB - USC 8; Yale 5. RBIs - Fitzgerald, Felske, Jones. W - Hood. L - Duffus. T - 2:02. A - 2,500. U - William McKinley, Fred Spurgeon.

Second Game, June 26, 1948

Southern California	ab	r	h	Yale	ab	r	h
Jones, cf	3	1	2	Moher, ss	5	2	3
Mazmanian, 2b	4	0	2	Goodyear, rf	3	1	1
Brideweser, ss	4	0	1	Breen, rf	1	0	0
Workman, lf	4	0	0	Redden, cf	4	1	2
Zuber, c	3	0	1	Mathews, 3b	5	2	2
Henley, rf	5	1	1	Fitzgerald, lf	2	1	0
Lillie, 3b	4	0	0	Felske, c	5	0	1
Cecillos, 1b	4	0	0	Bush, 1b	5	0	1
Kipp, p	2	0	0	Smith, 2b	5	1	2
Horst, p	0	0	0	Quinn, p	4	0	0
McKelvey, ph	1	0	1				
Freeman, ph	0	1	0				
Totals	39	3	8	Totals	34	8	12

Yale 202 020 110 - 8
Southern California 000 000 210 - 3

2B - Brideweser. 3B - Henley. S - Goodyear. SB - Moher, Redden. SO - by Quinn 6, by Kipp 3. BB - off Quinn 9, off Kipp 4, off Horst 1. HBP - by Quinn 1 (Workman). HO - Kipp 10 in 7, Horst 2 in 2. W - Quinn. L - Kipp. LOB - USC 14; Yale 11. RBIs - Bush 2, Smith, Mathews, Moher, Brideweser 2. T - 2:27. A - 3,000. U - William McKinley, Fred Spurgeon.

Third Game, Saturday, June 26, 1948

Southern California	ab	r	h	Yale	ab	r	h
Jones, cf	6	0	1	Moher, ss	5	0	1
Mazmanian, 2b	3	1	3	Breen, rf	1	0	0
Brideweser, ss	5	0	1	Marshall, c	2	1	1
Workman, lf	4	1	0	Felske, c	3	0	1
McKelvey, c	4	1	0	Redden, cf	4	0	3
Henley, rf	3	2	0	Mathews, 3b	4	1	1
Lillie, 3b	3	1	2	Lambert, 3b	0	0	0
Cecillos, 1b	3	2	1	Fitzgerald, lf	4	0	1
Bishop, p	5	1	2	Bush, 1b	4	0	1
Totals	36	9	10	Smith, 2b	4	0	0

Abbreviations
A - attendance
ab - at-bats
BB - base on balls
BK - balk
DP - double plays
E - errors
h - hits
HBP - hit by pitch
HR - home run
HO - hits off
IP - innings pitched
L - losing pitcher
LOB - left on base
PB - passed ball
R - runs
RBI - runs batted in
S - sacrifice
SB - stolen base
SF - sacrifice fly
SO - strikeouts
SV - save
T - time
U - umpires
W - winning pitcher
WP - wild pitch
2B - two-base hit
3B - three-base hit

	ab	r	h
Goodyear, p-rf	3	0	0
Kemp, p	1	0	0
Woodward, p	0	0	0
Duffus, p	0	0	0
Russ, c	0	0	0
James, ph	1	0	1
Rosenweig, cf	1	0	0
Totals	37	2	10

Southern California 141 000 030 - 9
Yale   000 101 000 - 2

2B - Bush, Redden. HR - Mathews. S - Mazmanian. SB - Workman. DP - Brideweser-Mazmanian- Cecillos. SO - by Kemp 1, by Woodward 2, by Bishop 3. BB - Goodyear 1, Kemp 1. LOB - USC 11, Yale 8. RBI - Bishop 2, Lillie 2, Jones, Brideweser, Workman, Cecillos, Mathews, Felske. HO - Goodyear, 4 in 1 (none out in second), Kemp 2 in 1, Woodward 3 in 6, Duffus, 1 in 1. W - Bishop. L - Goodyear. T - 2:19. A - 2,500. U - William McKinley, Fred Spurgeon.

1949

June 25, 1949

Texas	ab	r	h	Wake Forest	ab	r	h
Womack, lf	6	0	1	Hoch, ss	5	1	1
Hunt, ss	4	3	2	Hooks, 3b	3	1	0
Shamblin, 2b	6	3	5	Teague, 2b	5	0	3
Hamilton, 1b	5	2	2	Fulghum, lf	5	1	0
Kneuper, rf	5	1	3	Harris, rf	4	0	1
Brock, cf	5	0	0	Kersh, cf	2	0	0
Kana, 3b	5	1	2	Warren, 1b	3	0	0
Watson, c	5	0	2	Batchelor, c	3	0	0
Wall, p	2	0	1	Nicholas, p	2	0	1
Ehrler, p	2	0	0	Bauer, p	0	0	0
Totals	45	10	18	Rogers	1	0	0
				Mustian, p	0	0	0
				Wrenn	0	0	0
				Matney, 1b	0	0	0
				Livik	0	0	0
				Totals	33	3	6

Texas   110 020 240 - 10
Wake Forest 000 200 010 - 3

E - Hoch, Watson. RBI - Kneuper 2, Wall, Teague, Shamblin, Hamilton 4, Watson, Wrenn. 2B - Kana, Hoch, Shamblin, Hunt. 3B - Teague, Shamblin. HR - Hamilton. SB - Fulghum, Harris, Hooks. BB - Wall 0, Ehrler 4, Nicholas 4, Bauer 0, Mustian 0. SO - Wall 0, Ehrler 4, Nicholas 4, Bauer 0, Mustian 0. H - Wall 4 for 2 runs in 4 2/3; Nicholas 9 for 6 runs in 6; Ehrler 2 for 1 run in 4 1/3; Bauer 1 for 0 runs in 1; Mustain 8 for 4 runs in 2. HBP - Nicholas (Hunt), Ehrler (Hooks) (Batchelor). WP - Wall. W - Wall. SV - Ehrler. L - Nicholas. U - Brady, Carpenter, Massey, Paul.

Robert Brock played centerfield for Texas in 1949 and 1950.

The College World Series Record Book

1950

June 23, 1950

Washington St	ab	r	h	Texas	ab	r	h
McGuire, cf	4	0	0	Womack, lf	4	1	1
Carroll, 2b	3	0	0	Waghalter, 2b	0	1	0
Coleman, ss	4	0	3	Tompkins, ss	4	0	0
Tappe, 1b	4	0	1	Segrist, 1b	2	0	0
Brunswick, rf	2	0	0	Brock, cf	5	0	2
Paul, 3b	3	0	1	Kana, 3b	3	0	2
Carr, c	4	0	0	Hrncir, rf	3	1	0
Boytz, lf	2	0	0	Benson, c	3	0	1
Keogh, p	2	0	0	Ehrler, p	4	0	1
Conley, p	1	0	0	Wall, p	0	0	0
Watson, lf	1	0	0	Roberson pr	0	0	0
Totals	30	0	5		28	3	7

Washington State 000 000 000 - 0
Texas   000 102 00x - 3

RBI - Waghalter, Brock, Kana. 2B - Coleman. S - Waghalter. DP - Keough-Paul-Tappe, Kana-Waghalter-Segrist. LOB - Washington State 7, Texas 16. BB - Keogh 12, Conley 2, Ehrler 3, Wall 1. SO - Keough 4, Conley 5, Ehrler 8, Wall 2. HO - Keough, 6 in 5 2/3; Conley, 1 in 2 1/3; Ehrler, 4 in 7; Wall, 1 in 2. Balk - Keogh. PB - Benson 2. W -Ehrler. L - Keough. U - Soar, Warneki, Tobin. T - 2:32. A-2,384.

1951

June 17, 1951

Oklahoma	ab	r	h	Tennessee	ab	r	h
Wich, ss	5	0	1	Asbury, lf	3	0	2
Morgosh, 3b	3	1	1	Bell, ss	4	0	0
Sheets, 1b	5	0	2	Hopkins, 3b	4	0	1
Pugsley, cf	3	0	1	Hatfield, 1b-p	4	0	0
Antonio, rf	4	0	0	Rechichar, cf	4	0	0
McKee, lf	4	1	2	Anderson, c	2	1	0
Reddell, c	5	1	3	Payne, 2b	3	0	0
Harrah, 2b	4	0	0	Adams, rf	1	1	0
Shirley, p	3	0	1	Huffstetler, p	0	0	0
				Powell, 1b	2	0	0
Totals	36	3	11	Totals	27	2	3

Oklahoma   000 001 110 - 3
Tennessee 000 020 000 - 2

John Davis was a catcher on the Oklahoma team in 1951.

E - Rechichar. RBI - Morgosh, Pugsley, Reddell, Asbury, Powell. 2B - Hopkins, Reddell, Morgosh. 3B - McKee. SB - Reddell. S - Powell. DP - Wich-Sheets; Hatfield-Bell-Powell. LOB - Oklahoma 16, Tennessee 3. BB - Huffstetler 1, Hatfield 8, Shirley 4. SO - Hatfield 5, Shirley 6. HO - Huffstetler 1 in 1; Hatfield 10 in 8. HBP - Hatfield (Pugsley). WP - Hatfield 2. PB - Reddell 2. W - Shirley. L - Hatfield. U - Warneke, Tobin, Alvarez. T - 2:23. A - 6,290.

The College World Series Record Book

1952

June 17, 1952

Holy Cross	ab	r	h	Missouri	ab	r	h
Turco, lf	4	2	2	Dickinson, ss	5	1	1
Brissette, 2b	5	1	1	Kurtz, 2b	5	0	1
Moossman, cf	5	2	1	Monroe, lf	4	0	1
Concannon, ss	3	1	1	Wren, cf	5	0	0
Matrango, 3b	4	0	1	Patchett, rf	4	1	1
Hogan, rf	4	0	1	Lauer, 3b	4	0	1
Dyson, 1b	4	1	1	Sch'maker, 1b	4	2	2
Naton, c	4	1	0	Gellman, c	3	0	1
O'Neill, p	3	0	0	Atkinson, p	3	0	1
Totals	36	8	8	Beckman, p	0	0	0
				Soffer	1	0	0
				Totals	38	4	9

```
Holy Cross    120    000    302 - 8
Missouri      000    022    000 - 4
```

E - Brissette, Concannon, Dickinson, Wren, Lauer. RBI - Turco, Moossman, Concannon, Matrango 2, Hogan 2, Monroe, Schoonmaker 2, Atkinson. 3B - Schoonmaker. HR - Schoonmaker. SB - Turco. S - Dyson. LOB - Holy Cross 8, Missouri 9. BB - Atkinson 4, Beckman 2, O'Neill 2. SO - Atkinson 4, Beckman 1, O'Neill 9. HO - Atkinson 7 in 8, Beckman 1 in 1. PB - Gellman. W - O'Neill. L - Atkinson. U - Cibulka, Knapp, Pelton, Tobin. T - 2:34. A - 6,914.

1953

June 16, 1953

Texas	ab	r	h	Michigan	ab	r	h
Pace, 3b	5	0	1	Haynam, ss	5	1	2
Snow, lf	5	2	1	Mogk, 1b	3	1	0
Kelly, rf	4	1	2	Howell, cf	3	3	0
Eckert, cf	4	0	1	Eaddy, 3b	4	1	2
Oden, ss	5	1	2	Lepley, lf	5	1	2
Spradlin, c	3	1	2	Kline, rf	3	0	2
Mohr, 1b	4	0	1	Sabuco, 2b	4	0	0
Towery, 2b	4	0	1	Leach, c	3	0	1
Jungman, p	1	0	0	Wisniewski, p	2	0	0
Reifler, p	1	0	0	Corbett, p	0	0	0
Smith, p	2	0	0	Ritter, p	0	0	0
Biesenbach ph	1	0	0	Totals	32	7	9
Totals	39	5	11				

```
Texas       000    200    201 - 5
Michigan    002    300    02x - 7
```

E - Haynam, Howell, Smith 3, Mohr, Towery. RBI - Kelly, Eckert, Spradlin 3, Eaddy, Cline 2, Sabuco 2. 2B - Leach, Kelly 2, Lepley, Spradlin. 3B - Snow. HR - Spradlin. S - Wisniewski 2, Eaddy. LOB - Texas 12, Michigan 13. BB - Jungman 4, Reifler 1, Smith 4, Wisniewski 3, Corbett 2. SO - Reifler 3, Smith 1, Wisniewski 8, Ritter 1. HO - Jungman 4 in 2 1/3, Reifler 0 in 1, Smith 5 in 4 2/3, Wisniewski 11 in 8 (none out in ninth), Corbett 0 in 1/3, Ritter 0 in 2/3. R-ER - Jungman 2-2, Reifler 1-1, Smith 4-1, Wisniewski 5-3, Corbett 0-0, Ritter 0-0. LP - Reifler 2. W - Wisniewski. L - Jungman. U - Tobin, Dixon, Duffy, Luschen. T - 2:46. A - 5,303.

Abbreviations
A - attendance
ab - at-bats
BB - base on balls
BK - balk
DP - double plays
E - errors
h - hits
HBP - hit by pitch
HR - home run
HO - hits off
IP - innings pitched
L - losing pitcher
LOB - left on base
PB - passed ball
R - runs
RBI - runs batted in
S - sacrifice
SB - stolen base
SF - sacrifice fly
SO - strikeouts
SV - save
T - time
U - umpires
W - winning pitcher
WP - wild pitch
2B - two-base hit
3B - three-base hit

The College World Series Record Book

1954

June 16, 1954

Rollins	ab	r	h	Missouri	ab	r	h
Finnegan, c	4	0	1	Dickinson, ss	5	0	0
Talbot, 2b	4	0	0	Sickel, 3b	3	2	2
Butler, cf	4	0	0	Musgrave, rf	2	0	0
Helms, 3b	4	0	0	J. Schoonmaker, cf	4	0	1
MacHardy, 1b	3	1	1	Gleason, c	4	0	1
Smith, rf	3	0	1	R. Schoonmaker, 1b	3	1	0
Doran ph	1	0	0	Cox, 2b	1	1	1
Vancho, ss	3	0	1	Kammer, lf	3	0	1
Robinson, lf	3	0	0	Cook, p	4	0	0
Cary, p	0	0	0	Totals	29	4	6
Brophy, p	3	0	2				
Totals	32	1	6				

Rollins   000 100 000 - 1
Missouri   110 110 00x - 4

E - MacHardy, Robinson, Cox. RBI - Vancho, J. Schoonmaker, Gleason, Cox, Kammer. 2B - Brophy. HR - Cox. SB - Finnegan, Cox. S - Musgrave 2. DP - Dickinson-Cox-R. Schoonmaker. LOB - Rollins 5, Missouri 9. BB - Brophy 6, Cook 1. SO - Brophy 3, Cook 8. HO - Cary 3 in 2, Brophy 3 in 6. R-ER - Cary 2-2, Brophy 2-2, Cook 1-1. PB - Gleason. L - Cary. W - Cook. U - Chylak, Tobin, Hametz, Dixon. T - 1:53. A - 7,810.

1955

June 16, 1955

Wake Forest	ab	r	h	Western Michigan	ab	r	h
Moore, ss	6	0	1	Lajoie, cf	4	2	2
McKeel, cf	2	3	0	David, ss	4	1	1
Miller, rf	5	1	1	Johnson, rf	5	2	3
Holt, c	4	1	3	Nagel, lf	4	1	1
McRae, lf	5	2	5	Erickson ph	1	0	0
Barnes, 3b	3	0	0	Krings, 2b	3	0	0
Bryant, 2b	4	0	2	Czyz, 3b	3	0	0
Waggoner, 1b	3	0	0	Smith, 1b	2	0	0
Bonzagni, 1b	0	0	0	Messner, c	4	0	0
Walsh, p	1	0	0	Graham, p	1	0	0
Fichter, p	1	0	0	Schwartzkoff, p	3	0	1
McGinley, p	3	0	0	O'Connell ph	1	0	0
Cole	1	0	0	Bergman ph	1	0	0
Totals	38	7	12	Totals	36	6	8

Wake Forest   012 030 010 - 7
Western Michigan   003 300 000 - 6

E - Moore, Bryant, Czyz. RBI - Holt, McRae 3, Barnes, Bryant, Waggoner, Johnson 2, Nagel, Czyz. 2B - McRae, Lajoie, Bryant. SB - David, Johnson, Waggoner. S - Smith, Holt, Barnes. LOB - Wake Forest 12, Western Michigan 10. BB - Graham 2, Schwartzkoff 4, Walsh, 2, McGinley 4. HO - Graham 2 in 2 (faced 2 in 3rd), Schwartzkoff 9 in 7, Walsh 4 in 2 2/3, Fichter 1 in 1, McGinley 3 in 5 1/3. R-ER - Graham 3-3, Schwartzkoff 4-4, Walsh 3-3, Fichter 3-0, McGinley 0-0. PB - Messner 2. W - McGinley. L - Schwartzkoff. U - Doyle, Harbour, Hametz, Hergert. T - 2:45. A - 2,042.

Abbreviations
A - attendance
ab - at-bats
BB - base on balls
BK - balk
DP - double plays
E - errors
h - hits
HBP - hit by pitch
HR - home run
HO - hits off
IP - innings pitched
L - losing pitcher
LOB - left on base
PB - passed ball
R - runs
RBI - runs batted in
S - sacrifice
SB - stolen base
SF - sacrifice fly
SO - strikeouts
SV - save
T - time
U - umpires
W - winning pitcher
WP - wild pitch
2B - two-base hit
3B - three-base hit

The College World Series Record Book

1956

June 14, 1956

Arizona	ab	r	h	Minnesota	ab	r	h
Myers, cf	4	0	0	Horning, rf	5	3	4
Tomooka, ss	4	0	1	Lindblom, cf	5	1	2
McGinnis, 2b	3	1	2	Kindall, ss	4	1	1
Clarkson, rf	4	0	1	McCartan, 3b	5	2	1
Sorenson, 3b	4	0	0	Gillen, 1b	5	0	2
Messick, 1b	4	0	0	Anderson, lf	3	0	1
Chambers, lf	3	0	0	McNeeley, lf	2	0	0
Davis, c	2	0	1	Martin, 2b	3	2	1
Festin, c	1	0	0	Erickson, c	4	1	0
Oosterveen, p	1	0	0	Thomas, p	3	2	2
Hyman, p	1	0	0				
Boltz, p	1	0	0				
Totals	32	1	5	Totals	39	12	14

Arizona   000 001 000 - 1
Minnesota 300 160 20x - 12

R - McGinnis, Horning 3, Lindblom, Kindall, McCartan 2, Martin 2, R. Erickson, J. Thomas 2. E - McGinnis 2, Sorensen 2, Davis, Kindall. RBI - Horning 5, Lindblom, Gillen 2, R.P. Anderson, Martin, J. Thomas 2. 2B - Tomooka, Davis, Gillen, Kindall, Lindblom. 3B - J. Thomas. HR - Horning 2. DP - Toomoka-McGinnis-Messick, Sorensen-McGinnis-Tomooka. LOB - Arizona 5, Minnesota 6. BB - Oosterveen 3, J. Thomas 1. SO - Oosterveen 2, Hyman 1, Boltz 1, J. Thomas 4. HO - Oosterveen 4 in 3 1/3, Hyman 6 in 1 1/3, Blotz 4 in 3 1/3. R-ER - Oosterveen 4-4, Hyman 6-2, Boltz 2-2, J. Thomas 1-0. WP - Oosterveen, Hyman. PB - R. Erickson 2. W - J.Thomas (12-2). L - Oosterveen (6-3). U - Crawford, Tobin, Hametz, Tabacchi. T - 2:15. A - 3,890.

1957

June 12, 1957

Penn State	ab	r	h	California	ab	r	h
Baidy, 3b	5	0	0	Gregg, 2b	1	0	0
Hoover, 2b	5	0	1	Gaggero, 3b	4	0	1
Lockerman, cf	5	0	1	Robinson, ss	4	0	1
Stickler, c	3	0	0	Thompson, c	3	0	0
McMullen, rf	3	0	0	Puccinelli, rf	3	0	0
Tirabassi, ss	2	0	2	Reynolds, lf	3	0	0
Rainey, lf	4	0	0	Kelly, cf	2	1	0
Miller, 1b	4	0	1	Lavorel, 1b	3	0	0
Watkins, pr	0	0	0	Sterling, p	3	0	0
Emery, p	1	0	0	Totals	26	1	3
Totals	32	0	5				

Penn State 000 000 000 - 0
California 000 010 00x - 1

E - Hoover, Miller, Gaggero, Robinson, Gregg. RBI - Sterling. 2B - Hoover, Gaggero. 3B - Sterling. SB - Kelly 2. DP - Emery-Hoover. LOB - Penn State 12, California 5. BB - Sterling 7, Emery 4. SO - Sterling 5, Emery 9. R-ER - Emery 1-1. PB - Stickler. W - Sterling. L - Emery. U - Burkhart, Umont, Tobin, Harbour. T - 2:26. A - 3,211.

Abbreviations
A - attendance
ab - at-bats
BB - base on balls
BK - balk
DP - double plays
E - errors
h - hits
HBP - hit by pitch
HR - home run
HO - hits off
IP - innings pitched
L - losing pitcher
LOB - left on base
PB - passed ball
R - runs
RBI - runs batted in
S - sacrifice
SB - stolen base
SF - sacrifice fly
SO - strikeouts
SV - save
T - time
U - umpires
W - winning pitcher
WP - wild pitch
2B - two-base hit
3B - three-base hit

The College World Series Record Book

1958

June 19, 1958

Missouri	ab	r	h	rbi	Southern Cal	ab	r	h	rbi
Uriarte, 3b	5	0	3	2	Guffey, 1b	4	1	2	2
Grossman, cf	6	0	1	0	Siegert, rf	4	1	0	1
Starr, 2b	6	0	2	0	Blewett, 3b	2	0	1	1
Toft, rf	6	0	2	0	Castanon, 2b	6	1	1	0
Siebert, 2b	6	0	1	0	Fairly, cf	5	0	0	0
Hochgrebe, ss	6	2	1	0	Werhas, lf	5	0	1	1
Haas, lf	4	2	1	1	Heath, c	6	1	2	0
Kuhlmann, c	5	2	1	1	Scott, ss	4	1	1	1
Harbin, p	2	1	1	1	Biasotti, 3b	3	1	0	0
Gulick, p	1	0	0	0	Johnston, rf	2	1	1	0
Stehr, ph	1	0	0	0	Gardner, p	0	0	0	0
O'Donoghue, p	1	0	0	0	Blakeslee, p	4	1	1	1
Totals	49	7	13	5	Thom, p	1	0	0	0
					Totals	46	8	10	7

Missouri   040 000 030 000 - 7
Southern Cal   000 700 000 001 - 8

E - Starr 3, Toft, Hochgrebe, Harbin, Heath, Gardner. PO-A — Missouri 35-19, Southern Cal 36-15. DP - Hochgrebe-Starr-Siebert 2. LOB - Missouri 9, Southern Cal 13. 2B - Harbin, Uriarte, Kuhlmann. 3B - Haas. SB - Guffey. S - Guffey, Thom.

	IP	H	R	ER	BB	SO
Harbin	3	1	4	4	7	2
Gulick	4	6	3	3	0	2
O'Donoghue (L, 6-4)	4 2/3	3	1	1	2	1
Gardner	1	4	4	4	2	2
Blakeslee	6 2/3	8	3	3	1	4
Thom (W, 9-1)	4 1/3	1	0	0	0	2

WP - Gardner. U - Stewart, Smith, Carlton, Hametz. T-3:15. A-3,021.

1959

June 18, 1959

Oklahoma St	ab	r	h	rbi	Arizona	ab	r	h	rbi
B. Andrew, 2b	5	1	1	1	Hoffman, cf	4	1	1	1
McIlvoy, lf	3	1	1	1	Bubala, ph	1	0	0	0
R. Andrew, ss	3	0	0	0	Lewis, 2b	3	0	0	0
Dodson, 3b	4	1	2	1	Shoemaker, ss	4	0	1	1
Bond, c	3	0	0	1	Encinas, lf	3	0	1	0
Green, rf	4	0	1	0	Hall, c	3	1	1	0
Bancroft, cf	4	1	1	1	Wilson, 1b	4	0	1	0
Mersch, 1b	2	1	0	0	Ruiz, 3b	4	0	0	0
Bensinger, p	1	0	1	0	Fenderson, rf	2	1	1	1
R. Soergel, p	2	0	0	0	Baldwin, p	1	0	0	0
Totals	31	5	7	5	Popkin, p	1	0	0	0
					Totals	30	3	6	3

Oklahoma State 000 101 300 - 5
Arizona   000 111 000 - 3

E - Mersch, Ruiz. PO-A — Oklahoma State 27-13, Arizona 27-8. LOB -

All-Tournament Team

Sonny Siebert, Missouri, 1b
Mike Castanon, So. Cal, 2b
Ken Komodzinski, Holy Cross, 3b
Fred Scott, So. Cal, ss
Martin Toft, Missouri, of
Marvin Winegar, Western Mich., of
Ron Fairly, So. Cal, of
Hank Kuhlmann, Missouri, c
Bill Thorn, So. Cal, p
Doug Gulick, Missouri, p

USC's Bill Thorn was named most outstanding player in 1958.

All-Tournament Team

Bob Wilson, Arizona, 1b
Bruce Andrew, Oklahoma St., 2b
Jim Dobson, Oklahoma St., 3b
Charles Shoemaker, Arizona, ss
Doug Hoffman, Clemson, of
Bailey Hendley, Clemson, of
Connie McIlvoy, Oklahoma St., of

Oklahoma State 5, Arizona 8. 2B - Bensinger. 3B - B. Andrew. HR - Dodson, Bancroft. SB - Shoemaker. S - McIlvoy, Mersch, R. Soergel, Baldwin, Lewis. SF - Bond.

	IP	H	R	ER	BB	SO
Bensinger	3.2	3	1	1	3	5
Soergel (W, 8-1)	5.1	3	2	1	2	3
Baldwin (L, 10-2)	6.1	7	5	5	2	8
Popkin	2 .2	0	0	0	0	3

HBP - Soergel (Hall). Umpires-Stewart, Tobin, Carrothers, Sudol. T-2:35. A-4,168.

1960
June 20, 1960

So. Cal	ab	r	h	rbi	Minnesota	ab	r	h	rbi
Stillwell, ss	4	0	0	0	Causton, cf	4	0	1	0
Ryan, 1b	3	0	1	0	Junker, c	5	0	0	0
Satriano, 3b	4	0	1	0	Pflepsen, ss	5	1	1	0
Levingston, lf	4	0	0	0	Knapp, 1b	4	1	2	0
Heath, c	4	0	1	0	Erickson, 2b	4	0	1	0
Ersepke, rf	3	0	0	0	Nathe, lf	1	0	0	0
McNamee, cf	0	1	0	0	Haefner, lf	0	0	0	0
Bach, 2b	3	0	1	1	Moe, pr	0	0	0	0
Withers, p	3	0	0	0	Rolloff, 3b	3	0	1	2
Glassman, ph	1	0	0	0	Alford, rf	4	0	0	0
Yaryan, p	0	0	0	0	Rantz, p	3	0	1	0
Totals	29	1	4	1	Totals	33	2	7	2

Southern California 000 000 001 0 - 1
Minnesota 000 000 010 1 - 2

E - Rolloff. PO-A — So. Cal 28-13, Minnesota 30-15. DP - Pflepsen-Erickson-Knapp, Erickson-Pflepsen-Knapp. LOB - So. Cal 8, Minnesota 13. 2B - Knapp, Pflepsen. S - Stillwell, Knapp. SB - McNamee, Erickson.

Southern California	IP	H	R	ER	BB	SO
Withers	8	6	1	1	6	2
Yaryan (L, 5-2)	1.2	1	1	1	3	3
Minnesota						
Rantz (W, 4-2)	10	4	1	1	9	6

U - Summers, Carrothers, Yrkoski, LaBrosse. T - 2:33. A - 3,635.

1961
June 15, 1961

So. Cal.	ab	r	h	rbi	Ok. State	ab	r	h	rbi
Stillwell, ss	4	0	0	0	Wallace, ss	4	0	2	0
Gillespie, lf	4	1	1	0	Andrew, 2b	4	0	0	0
Satriano, 3b	4	0	2	0	McKenzie, cf	3	0	1	0
Ersepke, cf	4	0	1	1	Bond, c	3	0	0	0
Himes, c	4	0	1	0	Dodson, lf	3	0	0	0
McNamee, cf	4	0	0	0	Politte, rf	3	0	0	0
Bach, 2b	3	0	1	0	Karns, rf	0	0	0	0
Ryan, 1b	4	0	1	0	Ketchum, 3b	3	0	1	0
Withers, p	4	0	1	0	Mersch, 1b	3	0	0	0
					Fowler, p	2	0	0	0
					Wixson, p	1	0	0	0

Alan Hall, Arizona, c
Hal Stowe, Clemson, p
Joel Horlen, Oklahoma St., p

All-Tournament Team
William Ryan, So. Cal, 1b
John Erickson, Minnesota, 2b
Cal Rolloff, Minnesota, 3b
Dave Pflepsen, Minnesota, ss
Bob Levingston, So. Cal, of
Mickey McNamee, So. Cal, of
Art Ersepke, So. Cal, of
Bill Heath, So. Cal, c
Bruce Gardner, So. Cal, p
Bob Wasko, Minnesota, p
Jim Ward, Arizona, p

All-Tournament Team
William Ryan, So. Cal, 1b
Bruce Andrew, Oklahoma St., 2b
Dave Sarette, Syracuse, 3b
Don Wallace, Oklahoma St., ss
Bill Tomb, Western Mich., of
Don Davis, Duke, of

The College World Series Record Book

Totals	35	1	8	1	Totals	29	0	4	0

Southern California   000 000 010 - 1
Oklahoma State   000 000 000 - 0

E-Ketchum. PO-A–So. Cal. 27-6, Oklahoma State 27-13. DP-Andrew-Mersch. LOB-So. Cal. 8, Oklahoma State 2. 2B-Gillespie. 3B-Withers.

Southern California	IP	H	R	ER	BB	SO
Withers (W, 12-1)	9	4	0	0	0	13
Oklahoma State						
Fowler (L, 7-1)	7.2	8	1	1	1	4
Wixson	1.1	0	0	0	0	1

U-Foreman, Carrothers, Yrkoski, LaBrosse. T-2:03. A-,704.

Art Ersepke, So. Cal, of
Larry Himes, So. Cal, c
Littleton Fowler, Oklahoma St., p
Jim Withers, So. Cal, p
Larry Hankhammer, So. Cal, p

1962
June 16, 1962

Michigan	ab	r	h	rbi	Santa Clara	ab	r	h	rbi
Jones, 2b	5	0	0	0	McDermott, cf	3	0	2	1
Honig, ss	6	1	2	1	Giovanola, 2b	6	0	1	0
Tate, rf	6	0	1	0	Fazio, ss	7	1	0	0
Steckley, lf	6	0	1	0	Boccabella, 1b	6	2	3	0
Spalla, cf	6	1	1	0	Cullen, 3b	6	0	2	3
Merullo, c	6	0	0	0	Flanagan, lf	5	1	0	0
Campbell, 1b	6	0	0	0	Arrieta, rf	3	0	1	0
Chapman, 3b	5	2	1	0	DiBono, rf	3	0	0	0
Fisher, p	3	0	2	2	Calcagno, c	5	0	1	0
Bobel, p	2	1	1	1	Marcenaro, p	2	0	0	0
					Garibaldi, p	2	0	0	0
Totals	51	5	9	4	Totals	45	4	10	4

Michigan   000 100 200 000 002 - 5
Santa Clara   010 020 000 000 001 - 4

E - Honig, Merullo, Calcagno. PO-A — Michigan, 45-18, Santa Clara, 45-22. DP - Spalla-Honig-Jones, Honig-Jones-Campbell, Bobel-Honig-Campbell, Giovanoia-Fazio-Boccabella. LOB - Michigan 4, Santa Clara 12. 3B - Spalla, Fisher, Bobel. HR - Honig. SB - Jones, Steckley, Chapman. S - McDermot, Cullen, Arrieta. SF - McDermott.

	IP	H	R	ER	BB	SO
Fisher	9	8	3	2	4	11
Bobel (W, 4-2)	6	2	1	0	3	4
Marcenaro	7	7	3	3	2	5
Garibaldi (L, 10-3)	8	2	2	2	2	11

HBP - Fisher (Flanagan, Marcenaro). WP - Bobel, Garibaldi. U - Weyer, Carrothers, Yrkoski, LaBrosse. T - 3:32. A - 7,395.

All-Tournament Team

Dave Campbell, Michigan, 1b
Pat Rigby, Texas, 2b
Harvey Chapman, Michigan, 3b
Ernie Fazio, Santa Clara, ss
Ron Tate, Michigan, of
Ken Flanagan, Santa Clara, of
Mickey McDermott, Santa Clara, of
Joe Merullo, Michigan, c
Tom Belcher, Texas, p
Bob Garibaldi, Santa Clara, p

1963
June 16, 1963

Arizona	ab	r	h	rbi	Southern Cal	ab	R	h	rbi
Hawgood, cf	4	0	1	0	Brown, cf	3	2	2	0
Maxwell, ss	5	0	0	0	Holman, 1b	4	1	1	2
Theobold, 2b	4	1	3	0	Washington, lf	4	0	1	1
Morrison, rf	4	1	1	1	Thompson, rf	3	0	1	0
Brown, lb	2	0	0	0	Hill, lf	1	0	0	0

All-Tournament Team

Gary Holman, So. Cal, 1b
Ron Thoebald, Arizona, 2b
Dale Harvey, Missouri, 3b

27

The College World Series Record Book

Long, 1b	1	0	0	0	Hollowell, c	4	1	2	1	William Woodward,
Barnetche, lf	4	0	2	0	Dedeaux, 2b	3	1	1	0	Florida State, ss
Acuna, 3b	1	0	0	0	Walker, ss	3	0	0	0	Kenny Washington,
Patera, c	3	0	0	1	Sandel, 3b	3	0	1	1	So. Cal, of
Scott, p	2	0	0	0	Peterson, p	3	0	0	0	Craig Morrison,
Holliker, p	1	0	0	0						Arizona, of
Saull, ph	1	0	0	0						Hector Barnetche,
Totals	32	2	7	2	Totals	31	5	9	5	Arizona, of

Arizona 100 002 000 - 2
Southern Cal 120 020 00x - 5

E - Patera, Hill. PO-A – Arizona 24-10; Southern Cal 27-9. DP - Acuna-Thoebald-B. Brown; Maxwell-Theobald-Long; Walker-Dedeaux-Holman. LOB-Arizona 9, Southern Cal 4. 3B - W. Brown. HR - Hollowell, Holman. SB - Dedeuax, Hollowell.

Bud Hollowell, So. Cal, c
Walt Peterson, So. Cal, p
Doug Holliker, Arizona, p

	IP	H	R	ER	BB	SO
Scott (L, 8-3)	4.1	6	5	4	2	2
Holliker	3.2	3	0	0	0	4
Peterson (W, 12-2)	9	7	2	2	6	9

PB - Hollowell. U - Steiner, Carrothers, Kiehm, Labrosse. T - 2:23. A - 5,682.

1964
June 18, 1964

Minnesota	ab	r	h	rbi	Missouri	ab	r	h	rbi
Markus, 2b	4	0	1	0	Harvey, 3b	3	0	0	0
Hoffman, lf	4	0	0	0	Estes, ss	3	0	1	0
Davis, 1b	3	1	0	0	Woods, lf	3	0	1	0
Wojciak, c	3	0	0	0	Jim Sevcik, rf	4	0	1	0
Cawley, 3b	5	1	0	0	Price, 1b	4	0	0	0
Brousseau, rf	3	1	1	1	Simmons, ss	3	1	0	0
Clark, cf	3	0	0	0	Robbin, 2b	0	0	0	0
McCullough, ss	2	1	1	1	Strode, 2b	3	0	0	0
Pollack, p	4	1	2	1	John Sevcik, c	4	0	1	1
					Stroud, p	1	0	0	0
					Nelson, p	0	0	0	0
					Sigman, ph	0	0	0	0
					Sieck, p	0	0	0	0
					Rudanovich, ph	1	0	0	0
Totals	31	5	5	3	Totals	30	1	4	1

Minnesota 022 100 000 - 5
Missouri 010 000 000 - 1

E - Jim Sevcik, Simmons, Robben, Strode. 2B - Brousseau. 3B - McCullough. S - Clark 2, Hoffman.

	IP	H	R	ER	B	SO
Pollack (W, 11-2)	9	4	1	1	6	7
Stroud (L, 8-2)	3	4	5	1	3	3
Nelson	4	1	0	0	5	7
Steck	2	0	0	0	2	2

WP-Nelson, PB-John Sevcik. T-2:37. A-10,562.

All-Tournament Team
Bill Davis, Minnesota, 1b
Dewey Markus, Minnesota, 2b
Dave Thompson, Maine, 3b
Gary Sutherland, So. Cal, ss
Dan Hoffman, Minnesota, of
Gary Woods, Missouri, of
Willie Brown, So. Cal, of
Ron Wojciak, Minnesota, c
Joe Ferris, Maine, p
Joe Pollack, Minnesota, p

The College World Series Record Book

1965
June 12, 1965

Ohio State	ab	r	h	rbi	Arizona State	ab	r	h	rbi
Graham, 3b	3	0	0	0	Smith, lf	4	0	0	0
Copp, 3b	1	0	0	0	Dyer, rf	4	0	1	0
Reef, rf	4	0	0	0	Monday, cf	4	1	1	1
Rein, ss	3	0	0	0	Bando, 3b	3	1	2	0
Chonko, 1b	4	1	1	0	Laguna, 2b	2	0	0	1
Harkins, lf	2	0	2	1	Kleinman, 1b	2	0	0	0
Nagelson, cf	2	0	0	0	Stadler, c	3	0	1	0
Brinkman, c	2	0	0	0	Armstrong, ss	3	0	0	0
Jacobs, 2b	4	0	0	0	Merrick, p	2	0	0	0
Kitchton, p	1	0	0	0	Nurnberg, p	1	0	0	0
Shoup, ph	0	0	0	0					
Arlin, p	1	0	0	0					
Totals	27	1	3	1	Totals	28	2	5	2

Ohio State   000 100 000 - 1
Arizona State   100 001 00x - 2

E - Chonko, Bando 2. DP-Ohio State 1. LOB - Ohio State 8, Arizona State 5. 2B - Bando, Harkins. 3B-Bando. HR - Monday. S - Brinkman, Nagelson. SF - Lagunas.

	IP	H	R	ER	BB	SO
Kitchton (L, 4-3)	6	5	2	2	1	6
Arlin	2	0	0	0	0	2
Merrick (W, 13-2)	6	3	1	1	4	5
Nurnberg	3	0	0	0	2	4

T-2:02. A-5,698.

All-Tournament Team

Arnold Chonko, Ohio State, 1b
Luis Lagunas, Arizona State, 2b
Sal Bando, Arizona State, 3b
Bo Rein, Ohio State, ss
Rick Monday, Arizona State, of
Bob Fry, Washington St., of
Jim Dix, St. Louis, of
Chuck Brnkman, Ohio State, c
Steve Arlin, Ohio State, p
Doug Nurnberg,

1966
June 13, 1966

Oklahoma St	ab	r	h	rbi	Ohio State	ab	r	h	rbi
Spyres, ss	3	1	1	0	Shoup, rf	4	0	0	0
Sellari, c	4	0	0	0	Copp, 3b	4	2	3	1
Johnson, cf	4	0	1	0	Rein, lf	4	1	1	0
Toney, 3b	4	0	1	1	Nagelson, 1b	3	1	2	3
Weatherly, lf	4	0	2	0	Baker, cf	4	1	0	0
Kuykendall, rf	3	0	0	0	Sexton, ss	4	2	1	0
Keely, ph	1	0	0	0	Brinkman, c	4	1	0	0
McCord, 1b	4	1	2	1	Heine, 2b	3	0	2	0
Freeny, 2b	4	0	1	0	Boggs, p	3	0	0	0
Warrington, p	0	0	0	0	Swain, p	0	0	0	0
Burchart, p	3	0	0	0	Monroe, ph	1	0	0	0
					Arlin, p	0	0	0	0
Totals	34	2	8	2	Totals	34	8	9	6

Oklahoma State   000 000 110 - 2
Ohio State   301 002 02x - 8

E - Spyres, Freeny, Burchart. DP - Oklahoma State 2, Ohio State 1. LOB - Oklahoma State 6, Ohio State 7. 2B - Toney, Rein. 3B - Nagelson 2, Sexon. HR - McCord.

	IP	H	R	ER	BB	SO
Warrington (L, 2-1)	.1	3	3	2	0	0

All-Tournament Team

Russ Nagelson, Ohio State, 1b
Matt Galante, St.John's, 2b
Bob Toney, Oklahoma St., 3b
Joe Russo, St. John's, ss
Ray Shoup, Ohio State, of
Wayne Weatherly, Oklahoma St., of
Bo Rein, Ohio State, of
Chuck Brinkman, Ohio State, c
Steve Arlin, Ohio State, p
John Stewart, So. Cal, p

Burchart	7.2	6	5	2	5	9
Boggs (W, 6-1)	7	7	2	2	1	7
Swain	1	1	0	0	0	2
Arlin	1	1	0	0	0	1

T-2:25. A-10,507.

1967
June 12, 1967

Houston	ab	r	h	rbi	Arizona State	ab	r	h	rbi
Lucas, cf	5	2	3	0	Nelson, 2b	5	1	0	0
Baker, 2b	5	0	1	0	Reid, rf	3	4	2	2
Cantu, 3b	4	0	3	1	Carpenter, lf	5	1	2	2
Paciorek, lf	5	0	1	0	Paulson, 1b	4	1	1	1
Hebert, 1b	4	0	1	1	Grangaard, 3b	5	1	2	1
Burris, rf	5	0	1	0	Linville, cf	5	1	2	2
Toombs, ss	3	0	1	0	Lind, ss	3	0	0	1
Strelau, c	1	0	1	0	Davini, c	3	1	1	1
Silman, c	1	0	0	0	Burgess, p	4	1	0	0
Moore, p	0	0	0	0					
W. Hill, p	0	0	0	0					
B. Hill, p	3	0	0	0					
Williams, ph	1	0	0	0					
Totals	37	2	12	2	Totals	37	11	10	10

Houston   100 000 001 - 2
Arizona State 310 004 12x - 11

E - Baker, Cantu, Toombs (3), Strelau, Carpenter, Paulson. DP - Arizona State 1. LOB - Houston, 13, Arizona State, 9. 2B - Paciorek, Paulson, Reid. 3B - Cantu (2). SB - Grangaard, Lind. SF - Hebert.

	IP	H	R	ER	BB	SO
Moore (L, 3-2)	.2	2	3	3	2	0
W. Hill	0	0	0	0	2	0
B. Hill	6.1	7	6	2	2	5
Smith	1	1	2	0	1	0
Burgess (W, 16-3)	9	12	2	2	4	15

Time - 2:45. A - 9,210.

All-Tournament Team
Mark Marquess, Stanford, 1b
Dick Swan, Stanford, 2b
Dave Grangaard, Arizona State, 3b
Jack Lind, Arizona State, ss
Ike Lucas, Houston, of
Tom Paciorek, Houston, of
Scott Reid, Arizona State, of
Ron Davini, Arizona State, p
Q.V. Lowe, Auburn, p

1968
June 10, 1968

So. Illinois	ab	r	h	rbi	So. California	ab	r	h	rbi
Bond, cf	5	2	2	0	Ramshaw, ss	4	0	1	0
Rogad'ski, rf	4	0	1	1	Sooge, c	4	0	1	0
Kirkland, ss	3	1	1	1	Harrison, 2b	4	0	0	0
O'Sullivan, 3b	4	0	0	0	Homik, lf	4	1	1	0
Brumfield, 2b	3	0	1	1	Braden, rf	3	1	1	0
Blakley, lb	0	0	0	0	Seinsoth, 1b	4	1	2	2
Clark, 3b	2	0	1	0	Drake, 3b	4	0	1	0
Smith, lf	4	0	0	0	Brown, cf	4	0	1	0
Coker, c	4	0	1	0	Jaffe, cf	1	0	0	0
Paetzhold, p	1	0	0	0	McCombs, ph	1	1	1	0
Sedik, ph	1	0	0	0	Lee, p	3	0	1	0
Ash, p	0	0	0	0	Strom, p	0	0	0	0

All-Tournament Team
Bill Seinsoth, So. Cal, 1b
Lou Bagwell, Texas, 2b
Barry O'Sullivan, So. Ill., 3b
Danny Thompson, Okla. St., ss
Wayne Weatherly, Okla. St., of
Jerry Bond, So. Ill. of
Mike Rogodzinski,

The College World Series Record Book

Pitlock p	1	0	0	0	Kruchner ph	1	0	1	2
Totals	32	3	7	3	Totals	35	4	11	4

Southern Illinois   101 000 010 - 3
Southern California   000 200 002 - 4

E - Harrison, Drake. DP - Southern California 2. LOB - Southern Illinois 7, Southern California 6. 2B - Bond, Sogges, Drake. 3B - Kuehner. HR - Seinsoth (6), Kirkland (5). SB - Ramshaw, Lee.

	IP	H	R	ER	BB	SO
Paetzhold	6	6	2	2	0	2
Ash	.1	1	0	0	0	1
Pitlock (L, 4-3)	2.1	4	3	2	1	0
Lee	7.2	7	3	2	4	6
Strom (W, 12-4)	1.1	0	0	0	0	2

HBP-Lee, Blakley. PB-Coker. T-2:25. A-9,412.

So. Ill., of
Ralph Addonizio,
  St. John's, c
Bill Lee,
  So. Cal, p
Tom Sowinski,
  St. John's, p

1969
June 20, 1969

Tulsa	ab	r	h	rbi	Arizona State	ab	r	h	rbi
Whitaker lf	4	0	2	0	Detter ss	4	1	0	0
Jenkins cf	4	0	0	0	Dick rf	5	2	3	1
L. Rogers 3b	4	0	0	0	Dolinsek, lf	5	3	3	2
Caves 1b	4	1	1	0	Powell cf	4	2	3	1
Murphy c	3	0	1	1	Cotton c	4	2	1	3
Klahr c	0	0	0	0	Osborn lb	3	0	1	1
Adams 1b	3	0	0	0	Randle 2b	4	0	0	0
Honecutt ss	3	0	0	0	Valley 3b	3	0	0	0
Byrd rf	3	0	1	0	Gura p	4	0	0	0
Reetor rf	0	0	0	0					
Valley 3b	3	0	0	0					
Rothwell, pr	0	0	0	0					
Totals	31	1	6	1	Totals	36	10	11	8

Tulsa   010 000 000 - 1
Arizona State 013 033 00x - 10

E - L. Rogers, Honeycutt. DP - Arizona St. 2. LOB - Tulsa 3, Arizona St. 6. 3B- Caves. HR - Dolinsek (9), Cotton (3). SB - Deter.

	IP	H	R	ER	BB	SO
S. Rogers (L, 8-1)	5.2	10	10	8	2	4
Butcher	2.1	1	0	0	0	3
Gura (W, 19-2)	9	6	2	1	0	10

WP - S. Rogers 3. HBP - S. Rogers (Powell), Butcher (Valley). U - Mcdonough, Newsome, Yost, Harvey. T - 1:39. A - 10,050.

All-Tournament Team
Steve Caves, Tulsa, 1b
Lou Bagwell, Texas, 2b
Les Rogers, Tulsa, 3b
Roger Detter, Arizona St., ss
John Dolinsek, Arizona St., of
Paul Powell, Arizona St., of
Jim Cardasis, New York U., of
Billy Cotton, Arizona St., c
Larry Gura, Arizona St., p
Burt Hooton, Texas, p

1970
June 12, 1970

Florida State	ab	r	h	rbi	Southern Cal	ab	r	h	rbi
Nichols, 2b	7	0	0	0	Cross, lf	3	0	1	0
Cocks, lf	6	0	0	0	Petersen, ph	3	0	0	0
Grubb, cf	6	0	2	0	Barr, p	3	0	0	0
Cash, 3b	6	0	1	0	Meier, ss	6	1	3	1
Saferight, c	5	0	1	0	Stoligrosz, 3b	6	0	0	0
G. Gromek, ss	6	0	0	0	Kingman, rf	7	0	1	0

All-Tournament Team
John Langerhans, Texas, 1b
Frank Alfano, So. Cal, 2b
Dan Stoligrosz, So. Cal, 3b
Jerry Lundin,

31

Kasimier, 1b	6	0	0	0	Alfano, 2b	7	0	3	1
Porter, rf	4	1	2	0	Perkins, c	6	0	1	0
Osburn, p	1	0	0	0	Carter, pr	0	0	0	0
Ammann, pr	0	0	0	0	Swid'ski, c	0	0	0	0
Ferguson, p	1	0	0	0	Ball, 1b	2	0	0	0
Slade, p	0	0	0	0	Arenstein, 1b	4	0	0	0
Scarce, p	2	0	1	0	Bennett, cf	6	0	0	0
C. Gromek, p	0	0	0	0	Widman, p	1	0	0	0
					Port, ph-lf	1	1	0	0
Totals	50	1	7	0	Totals	52	2	9	2

Florida State   000 010 000 000 000 - 1
Southern Cal   000 000 100 000 001 - 2

E - Grubb, Cash, Widman. DP - Southern Cal 2. LOB - Florida State 9; Southern Cal 15. 2B - Meier. SB - Grubb. S - Scarce

	IP	H	R	ER	BB	SO
Osburn	4	0	0	0	0	4
Ferguson	2.2	1	1	1	2	2
Slade	0	1	0	0	0	0
Scarce (L, 1-2)	7.1	1	1	1	3	9
C. Gramek	0	2	0	0	1	0
Widman	7	4	1	0	3	6
Barr (W, 14-2)	8	3	0	0	1	5

A-11,542. T-3:50.

1971

June 17, 1971

So. Illinois	ab	r	h	rbi	So. California	ab	r	h	rbi
Eden, 3b	3	0	0	0	Ambrow, ss	5	0	1	1
Dwyer, cf	4	1	1	0	Cross, lf	3	1	1	1
Kuiper, 2b	3	0	0	0	Pederson, lf	1	0	0	0
Thomas, 1b	4	0	1	0	Port, 3b	4	1	1	0
Radison, ss	4	1	2	0	Perkins, c	3	1	1	1
Calufetti, c	3	0	2	1	Alfano, 2b	3	2	2	3
Blakley, rf	3	0	0	1	Steele, rf	4	0	2	0
Liggett, lf	3	0	0	0	Carter, cf	3	0	0	0
Langdon, p	2	0	2	0	Artenstein, 1b	3	1	1	1
Broeking, p	0	0	0	0	Busby, p	4	1	1	0
Sedik, ph	1	0	0	0					
Randall p	0	0	0	0					
Totals	30	2	8	2	Totals	33	7	10	7

Southern Illinois   010 000 001 - 2
Southern California   002 120 20x - 7

E - Thomas, Calufetti. DP - Southern California 2. LOB - Southern Illinois 5, Southern California 6. HR - Perkins (9), Alfano (2). S - Blakley.

	IP	H	R	ER	BB	SO
Langdon (L, 12-2)	5.1	8	5	2	3	4
Broeking	1.2	2	2	2	0	1
Randall	1	0	0	0	1	1
Busby (W, 11-2)	9	8	2	2	3	6

T-2:44. A-13,945

Iowa State, ss
John Grubb,
 Florida State, of
Gary Shade,
 Ohio, of
Mike Markl,
 Texas, of
Tommy Harmon,
 Texas, c
Gene Ammann,
 Florida State, p
Jim Barr,
 So. Cal, p

All-Tournament Team

Jerry Tabb,
 Tulsa, 1b
Frank Alfano,
 So. Cal., 2b
Mike Eden,
 So. Ill., 3b
Dan Radison,
 So. Ill., ss
Fred Lynn,
 So. Cal, of
Steve Bowling,
 Tulsa, of
Jim Dwyer,
 So. Ill., of
Larry Calufetti,
 So. Ill., c
Mark Sogge,
 So. Cal, c
Steve Rogers,
 Tulsa, p

The College World Series Record Book

1972
June 16, 1972

So. Cal	ab	r	h	rbi	Arizona State	ab	r	h	rbi
Guggia, 2b	4	0	1	0	Wills, lf	2	0	1	0
Port, 3b	4	0	0	0	Reed, 2b	4	0	0	0
Lynn, cf	3	0	0	0	Atwell, cf	4	0	0	0
Ceci, c	4	0	0	0	Bannister, ss	4	0	1	0
Huizenga, lf	4	0	1	0	Myers, c	3	0	1	0
Smalley, ss	4	0	1	0	Valley, 3b	4	0	0	0
Steele, rf	4	1	2	0	Mantle, 1b	4	0	0	0
Arenstein, 1b	2	0	0	0	White, rf	3	0	1	0
Sogge, p	2	0	0	0	Glazebrk, ph	1	0	0	0
McQueen, p	1	0	0	0	Crawford, p	2	0	2	0
Totals	32	1	5	0	Totals	31	0	6	0

Southern California   001   000   000 - 1
Arizona State   000   000   000 - 0

E - Guggia, Mantle. DP - Southern California 3, Arizona State 1. LOB - Southern California 6, Arizona State 5. 2B - Steele. S - Crawford.

	IP	H	R	ER	BB	SO
Sogge	4	5	0	0	2	0
McQueen (W, 9-3)	5	1	0	0	1	5
Crawford (L, 13-2)	9	5	1	1	2	8

WP - Crawford. T - 2:05. A - 6,950.

All-Tournament Team

Daryl Arenstein, So. Cal, 1b
Ken Reed, Arizona State, 2b
David Chalk, Texas, 3b
Steve Dillard, Mississippi, ss
Bump Wills, Arizona State, of
Tim Steele, So. Cal, c
Russ McQueen, So. Cal, p
Craig Swan, Arizona State, p

1973
June 13, 1973

Southern Cal	ab	r	h	rbi	Arizona State	ab	r	h	rbi
Smalley, ss	4	1	1	0	Kendrick, lf	4	0	0	0
Dauer, 3b	4	0	0	0	Berger, 2b	4	0	0	0
Bowman, rf	4	2	2	1	Atwell, cf	3	2	2	0
Heizenga, lf	4	1	2	2	Harris, rf	4	1	2	1
Putman, c	4	0	0	0	Myers, c	4	0	0	0
Lynn, cf	4	0	2	1	Westlake, 1b	4	0	2	1
Adolph, 2b	3	0	2	0	Sain, 3b	2	0	0	0
Arnstein, 1b	2	0	0	0	Rawlings, ph	1	0	0	0
Barr, p	2	0	0	0	Oscarson, 3b	0	0	0	0
Reinke, p	1	0	0	0	White, ph	1	0	0	0
					Wills, ss	3	0	0	0
					Umbarger, p	1	0	0	0
					Slocum, p	2	0	1	0
Totals	32	4	9	4	Totals	32	3	7	2

Arizona State   000   201   000 - 3
Southern Cal   202   000   00x - 4

E - Myers, Slocum, Smalley. DP - Arizona State. LOB - Arizona State 4, Southern Cal 6. 2B - Smalley, Bowman, Huizenga, Adolph, Westlake. 3B - Slocum. S - Adolph.

	IP	H	R	ER	BB	SO
Umbarger (L, 5-3)	2.1	7	4	3	0	1
Slocum	5.2	2	0	0	1	7
Barr (W, 10-2)	5.1	7	3	3	1	4
Reinke	3.2	0	0	0	0	4

S - Reinke. U - Motley, Hollar, Threadgold, Agnes. WP - Barr, Reinke. T: 2:28. A-12,050.

All-Tournament Team

Clay Westlane, Arizona State, 2b
Bill Berger, Arizona State, 2b
Keith Moreland, Texas, 3b
Roy Smalley, So. Cal, ss
Terry Pyka, Texas, of
Carl Person, Ga. Southern, of
Ken Huizenga, So. Cal, of
Clint Meyers, Arizona State, c
Dave Winfield, Minnesota, p
Eddie Bane, Arizona State, p
Randy Scarbery, So. Cal, p
Bob Shirley, Oklahoma, p

The College World Series Record Book

1974

June 15, 1974

Southern Cal	ab	r	h	rbi	Miami (Fla.)	ab	r	h	rbi
Tevlin, rf	5	0	2	0	Crosta, 3b	3	0	0	1
Cobb, ss	5	1	1	0	Gonzalez, 1b	5	0	2	1
Dauer, 3b	5	1	1	1	Krenchicki,, ss	4	0	0	0
Kemp, dh	4	0	0	0	Reichie, dh	3	0	0	0
Putman, c	4	0	1	1	LoMedico, dh	0	0	0	0
Mitchell, lf	3	2	1	0	Vega, pr	0	0	0	0
Huizenga, cf	4	1	2	0	Truillo, cf	4	1	2	0
Carpenter, 1b	3	1	1	1	Castillo, 2b	4	0	1	0
Adolph, 2b	4	1	2	2	Scott, c	3	0	0	1
					D'Innocenzia, rf	2	1	1	0
					Stepe, lf	4	1	0	0
Totals	37	7	11	5	Totals	32	3	6	3

Southern California 030 002 200 - 7
Miami   000 100 200 - 3

E - Gonzalez, Adolph, Krenchicki, Cobb. DP - Southern Cal 1. LOB - Southern Cal 6, Miami 9. 2B - Tevlin, Dauer, Putman, Castillo. HR - Adolph (6). S - Carpenter. SB - Scott.

	IP	H	R	ER	BB	SO
Raccnelli	4	4	1	0	4	5
Milke (W, 6-3)	4	2	2	0	1	5
Jakubowski (L, 16-3)	7	10	7	3	2	7
Floyd	2	1	0	0	0	0

PB - Scott, Pulman. HBP - By Milke (LoMedico). T - 2:41. A - 11,346.

All-Tournament Team

Orlando Gonzalez, Miami, 1b
Rob Adolph, So. Cal, 2b
Rich Dauer, So. Cal, 3b
Marvin Cobb, So. Cal, ss
Manny Trujillo, Miami, of
Bob Mitchell, So. Cal, of
Tom Ball, Texas, of
Ron Scott, Miami, c
George Milke, So. Cal, p
Mark Barr, So. Cal, p
Stan Jakubowski, Miami, p

1975

June 11, 1975

Texas	ab	r	h	rbi	South Carolina	ab	r	h	rbi
Anderson, lf	4	1	1	1	Gantz, ss	4	0	1	0
Stouffer, ss	4	0	0	0	Hancock, rf	3	0	0	0
Moreland, 3b	5	1	1	1	Repsher, ph-rf	1	0	0	0
Bradley, rf	5	0	1	0	Small, 1b	4	1	1	1
Reichenbach, 1b	5	1	1	2	King, dh	4	0	0	0
Duncan, c	4	0	0	0	Pankovits, 2b	4	0	0	0
Griffin, dh	3	2	3	0	Cook, rf	3	0	1	0
Proske, cf	3	0	1	0	Keatley, c	2	0	0	0
Pyka, 2b	3	0	0	1	Fleming, lf	3	0	1	0
					VanBvr, 2b	3	0	0	0
Totals	36	5	8	5	Totals	31	1	4	1

Texas   012 100 010 - 5
South Carolina 000 100 000 - 1

E - Pankovits 2. LOB - Texas 9, South Carolina 4. 2B - Moreland. HR - Reichenbach (5), Small (19). S - Pyka.

	IP	H	R	ER	BB	SO
Wortham (W, 15-1)	9	1	1	1	1	9
Bass (L, 17-1)	8.2	8	5	3	4	8
Cromer	.1	0	0	0	0	0

T-2:20. A-10,717.

All-Tournament Team

Mickey Reichenbach, Texas, 1b
Mark Van Bever, So. Carolina, 2b
Gary Allenson, Arizona State, 3b
Blair Stouffer, Texas, ss
Bob Pate, Arizona State, of
Steve Cook, So. Carolina, of
Rick Bradley, Texas, of
Rick Cerone, Seton Hall, c
Earl Bass, South Carolina, p
Richard Wortham, Texas, p

The College World Series Record Book

1976
June 11, 1976

Eastern Mich.	ab	r	h	rbi	Arizona	ab	r	h	rbi
Brier, dh	4	0	1	0	Zimmerman, lf	4	2	1	0
Dasen, lf	4	0	0	0	Wendt, ss	4	2	2	0
Gulliver, ss	3	1	1	1	Stegman, cf	4	0	3	3
Keller, c	4	0	0	0	Hassey, c	4	0	2	1
Ambrose, 1b	3	0	2	0	Pearsey, 2b	5	0	1	0
Lauerman, cf	4	0	0	0	Van Horne, 1b	4	2	3	0
Boutin, rf	2	0	0	0	Bolek, rf	2	0	0	0
Petroff, 3b	3	0	1	0	Powers, dh	3	1	2	3
Schmitz, 2b	2	0	1	0	Simpson, 3b	4	0	0	0
Luckhardt, ph	1	0	0	0					
Carreri, 2b	0	0	0	0					
Totals	30	1	6	1	Totals	34	7	14	7

Eastern Michigan 000 000 001 - 1
Arizona   001 410 01x - 7

DP - Eastern Michgan 2, Arizona 1. LOB - Eastern Michigan 5, Arizona 10. 2B - Stegman, Petroff. 3B - Stegman. HR - Powers, Gulliver. SB - Powers. SH - Bolek.

	IP	H	R	ER	BB	SO
Welch (L)	3 2/3	8	4	4	2	3
Owchinko	4 1/3	6	3	3	3	2
Chaulk (W)	9	6	1	1	3	5

WP - Owchinko 2. PB - Hassey. U - Mitchell, Neese, Cossey, Gerardi. T - 2:06. A - 11, 576.

All-Tournament Team

Ken Phelps, Arizona State, 1b
Dan Schmitz, E. Mich., 2b
Brian Petroff, E. Mich., 3b
Russ Quetti, Maine, ss
Dave Stegman, Arizona, of
Ken Landreaux, Arizona State, of
Pete Van Horne, Arizona, of
Ron Hassey, Arizona, c
Steve Powers, Arizona, dh
Bob Owchinko, E. Mich., p
Bob Chaulk, Arizona, p

1977
June 10, 1977

South Carolina	AB	R	H	RBI	Arizona State	ab	r	h	rbi
Vn Bvr, 2b	4	0	0	0	Peters, cf	4	1	2	0
Wilson, cf	4	0	1	0	Hendersen, ss	3	0	2	0
McLean, lf	4	0	0	0	Allen, dh	4	0	0	0
Rensher, rf	4	0	0	0	Horner, 2b	3	0	0	0
King, dh	4	1	1	1	Bando, c	3	1	1	1
Hinkel, 1b	3	0	1	0	Michael, lf	3	0	1	0
Murphy, 3b	3	0	1	0	Myman, 1b	3	0	0	0
Long, c	3	0	1	0	Humphrey, 3b	3	0	1	0
Jonson, ss	3	0	0	0	Brooks, rf	3	0	0	0
Lewis, p	0	0	0	0					
Totals	32	1	5	1	Totals	29	2	7	1

South Carolina 000 000 100 - 1
Arizona State   001 000 10x - 2

E - Lewis, Jonson 2, Vasquez. DP - South Carolina 1. LOB - South Carolina 4, Arizona State 4. 2B - Hinkel. HR - King (5), Bando (9). SB - Peters 2.

	IP	H	R	ER	BB	SO
Lewis (L, 11-6)	8	7	2	2	1	7
Vasquez (W, 12-2)	9	5	1	1	0	3

T,-,1:35. A,-,11,876.

All-Tournament Team

Chris Nyman, Arizona State, 1b
Bob Horner, Arizona State, 2b
Brandt Humphry, Arizona State, 3b
Mike Henderson, Arizona State, ss
Chuck McLean, South Carolina, lf
Mookie Wilson, South Carolina, cf
David Caldwell, Clemson, rf
Steve Stieb, So. Ill., c
Jamie Allen, Arizona State, p
Jerry Vasquez, Arizona State, p
Randy Martz, South Carolina, p

The College World Series Record Book

1978
June 18, 1978

Southern Cal	AB	R	H	RBI	Arizona State	ab	r	h	rbi
Wells, cf	5	0	0	0	Irvine, cf	5	0	1	0
Strokke, ss	5	1	2	1	Michael, rf	5	1	3	0
Smith, dh	6	1	1	1	Brooks, ss	4	0	2	0
Tolman, lf	5	1	3	1	Horner, 3b	4	1	0	0
Hostetler, 1b	5	2	3	2	Bando, c	4	1	1	2
Engle, 3b	5	1	1	0	Allen, 2b	3	0	2	1
Brown, cf	3	2	2	0	Anicich, 1b	2	0	0	0
Fobbs, 2b	5	1	2	3	Moon, ph	1	0	0	0
Van Gorder, c	4	0	2	2	Stahl, lf	1	0	0	0
					Hudgens, dh	2	0	0	0
					Eller, p	2	0	0	0
Totals	43	10	16	10	Totals	33	3	9	3

Southern Cal   032 002 030 -10
Arizona State   000 000 030 - 3

E - Brooks, Allen, Stahl. DP - Southern Cal 3. LOB - Southern Cal 12, Arizona State 10. 2B - Brown, Fobbs, Bando, Allen. HR - Hostetler. SF - Van Gorder.

Arkansas	IP	H	R	ER	BB	SO
Bordley (W, 12-2)	7.1	7	3	3	6	1
Schaffinger	1.2	2	0	0	1	1
Arizona State						
Dean (L, 6-4)	2.1	6	5	5	3	0
Vasquez	2.2	8	2	2	0	0
Eller	3	2	3	3	2	1
Hawk	1	0	0	0	0	0

T-2:32. A-12,172.

All-Tournament Team
Dave Hostetler, So. Cal, 1b
Mike Fox, No. Carolina, 2b
Bob Horner, Arizona State, 3b
Doug Stokke, So. Cal, ss
Tim Tolman, So. Cal, lf
John Wells, So. Cal, cf
Steve Michael, Arizona State, rf
Chris Bando, Arizona State, c
Randy Guerra, Miami, dh
Rod Boxberger, So. Cal, p
Casey Lindsey, Arizona State, p

1979
June 1, 1979

Arkansas	ab	r	h	rbi	Fullerton State	ab	r	h	rbi
Ray, 2b	3	0	1	0	Favato, dh	4	1	0	0
L Wilce, ss	4	0	2	1	Palmer, rf	2	0	0	0
E Wilce, dh	3	0	0	0	Wilch, 1b	1	0	0	1
McReynolds, cf	4	0	0	0	Hanggie, 3b	3	0	1	0
Hennell, 1b	4	0	0	0	Velor, lf	3	0	0	0
Brumble, lf	4	0	1	0	Garrett, lf	0	0	0	0
Reynolds, c	4	0	0	0	Kingsolver, c	3	0	1	0
Ash, rf	2	0	0	0	Garcia, 2b	3	1	1	0
Martin, rf	1	0	0	0	Robertson, ss	3	0	0	0
Kauffman, 3b	2	1	0	0					
Totals	31	1	4	1	Totals	3	0	2	1

Arkansas   000 010 000 - 1
Fullerton State 000 011 00x - 2

E - Reynolds, Kauffman. DP - Arkansas 2. LOB - Arkansas 6, Fullerton St.-2. SB - Hanggie, Favata. SF - Wallach.

	IP	H	R	ER	BB	SO
Krueger (L, 10-2)	8	5	2	1	2	5
Worthman (W, 15-2)	9	4	1	1	3	4

All-Tournament Team
Tim Wallach, Cal St. Ful., 1b
Mike Gates, Pepperdine, 2b
Dan Hanggie, Cal St. Ful., 3b
Larry Wallace, Arkansas, ss
Marc Brumble, Arkansas, lf
Kevin McReynolds, Arkansas, cf
Matt Vejar, Cal St. Ful., rf
Kurt Kingsolver, Cal St. Ful., c
Keith Walker, Texas, dh
Tony Hudson, Cal St. Ful., p
Steve Krueger, Arkansas, p

The College World Series Record Book

1980

June 6, 1980

Hawaii	ab	r	h	rbi	Arizona	ab	r	h	rbi
Bass, cf	5	0	1	0	Taylor, rf	5	0	2	1
Reece, 2b	5	1	1	0	Moses, cf	4	0	1	0
Tanabe, c	4	2	3	0	Francona, lf	4	0	0	0
Erdahl, lf	5	0	0	0	Clements, 1b	4	1	3	0
Kakazu, dh	4	0	1	0	Stanley, dh	4	1	2	1
Lono, pr	0	0	0	0	Quick, 2b	2	0	0	0
Perkins, 3b	4	0	2	2	Candaele, 3b	4	1	1	0
Williams, rf	4	0	1	0	Crist, ss	3	2	2	1
Dashefsky, 1b	3	0	1	0	Hyman, c	3	0	1	1
Tokunaga, ss	4	0	0	0					
Totals	38	3	10	2	Totals	33	5	12	4

Hawaii   000 100 200 - 3
Arizona   010 301 00x - 5

E - Reece, Tanabe, Erdahl, Dashefsky, Candaele, Hyman. LOB - Hawaii 10, Arizona 9. 2B - Clements 2, Stanley, Crist. SB - Williams, Taylor. CS - Francona, Taylor. SH - Quick.

	IP	H	R	ER	BB	SO
Smith (L)	3.2	8	4	4	1	1
Olmos	3.0	3	1	0	1	3
Kakazu	0.2	1	0	0	0	1
Duquette	0.2	0	0	0	0	1
Lefferts (W)	6.2	10	3	1	2	2
Barger (S)	2.1	0	0	0	0	2

WP - Lefferts, Olmos. HBP - by Olmos (Crist, Hyman). U - Bible, Patch, Mauer, Clements. T-2:41. A-15,276.

All-Tournament Team

Wes Clements, Arizona, 1b
Paul Hundhammer, Miami (Fla.), 2b
Kimo Perkins, Hawaii, 3b
Eric Tokunaga, Hawaii, ss
Terry Francona, Arizona, lf
Lyle Brackenridge, California, cf
Jim Paciorek, Michigan, rf
Collin Tanabe, Hawaii, c
Paul Maruffi, St. John's (N.Y.), dh
Crain Lefferts, Arizona, p
Greg Barber, Arizona, p

1981

June 8, 1981

Oklahoma St	ab	r	h	rbi	Arizona State	ab	r	h	rbi
Baughn, cf	3	0	0	0	Miller, cf	5	2	2	0
Tettleton, rf	3	2	1	0	Siebert, cf	0	0	0	0
Dilks, dh	2	1	0	1	Hill, ss	3	1	1	0
Roth, ph	0	0	0	0	Nelson, rf	3	1	0	0
Traber, 1b	4	0	1	1	Romine, ph	2	1	2	0
Etchebarren, 2b	3	1	0	1	Sodders, 3b	3	1	0	1
Del Rosa, lf	3	0	0	0	Davis, 1b	5	0	2	0
Dorn, ph	1	0	0	0	Holmes, lf	4	1	2	0
Poole, c	3	0	0	0	McCain, dh	2	0	1	1
Kastic, ss	3	0	0	0	Johnston, ph	2	0	0	0
Edwards, ph	1	0	1	1	Martinez, 2b	5	0	1	0
Cardnli, 3b	3	0	1	0	Wilson, c	4	0	2	0
Chadwick, p	1	0	0	0					
Totals	30	4	4	4	Totals	38	7	13	4

Oklahoma State 201 000 001 - 4
Arizona State   202 101 01x - 7

E - Dilks, Traber, Etchebarren, Poole, Hill. LOB - Oklahoma State 5, Arizona State 13. 2B - Traber, Edwards, Miller, Holmes. 3B - Tettleton, Miller. SB - Romine. SF - Sodders.

All-Tournament Team

Alvin Davis, Arizona State, 1b
Ray Etchebarren, Oklahoma St., 2b
Mike Sodders, Arizona State, 3b
Rod Carraway, So. Carolina, ss
Stan Holmes, Arizona State, of
Mickey Tettleton, Oklahoma St., of
Mark Gillaspie, Miss. St., of
Burk Goldthorn, Texas, c
Lemmie Miller, Arizona State, dh
Kevin Dukes, Arizona State, p

The College World Series Record Book

Oklahoma State	IP	H	R	ER	BB	SO
Coplon (L, 10-4)	3	6	5	4	3	1
Rodgers	2	2	1	0	0	1
Dilks	2	3	0	0	0	3
Jacques	.1	1	1	1	0	0
Lawrence	.2	1	0	0	1	0
Arizona State						
Carter	.1	2	2	1	0	1
Dukes (W, 8-2)	8.2	2	2	2	6	6

WP - Coplon, Dukes. HBP - By Coplon (Sodders). T - 3:03. A - 13,239.

Don Mundie, Miss. St., p

1982
June 12, 1982

Miami	ab	r	h	rbi	Wichita State	ab	r	h	rbi
Wrona, ss	3	1	2	1	Thomas, 2b	4	1	2	0
Lusby, 1b	4	1	1	1	Hibbs, cf	4	0	0	0
Sorce, dh	4	0	0	1	Stephenson, 1b	4	1	2	1
Lane, 3b	5	1	2	3	Morman, dh	5	1	2	2
Santovenia, c	3	1	1	0	O'Brien, c	4	0	0	0
Velazquez, lf	3	2	2	0	Spring, 3b	4	0	0	0
Seoane, 2b	4	1	2	0	Grogan, lf	4	0	0	0
Williams, rf	2	1	0	0	Gaskell, rf	2	0	0	0
Shields, cf	3	2	2	3	Lucas, ss	4	0	1	0
Carr, lf	1	0	0	0					
Totals	34	9	12	9	Total	35	3	7	3

Miami   000 061 020 - 9
Wichita State   201 000 000 - 3

E - Lusby, Williams, Spring. DP - Miami 1, Wichita State 2. LOB - Miami 2, Wichita State 2. 2B - Santovenia, Seoane, Thomas, Stephenson 2. HR - Lane (25), Morman (25). S - Williams. SF - Sorce. SB - Williams, Shields, Thomas

Miami	IP	H	R	ER	BB	SO
Kasprzak, (W, 14-4)	7	6	3	3	3	5
D. Smith (S, 3)	2	1	0	0	2	2
Wichita State						
Heinkel (L, 16-5)	5	5	7	7	5	7
Brown	2.1	6	2	1	2	0
Howerton	.2	1	0	0	0	1
LaFever	1	0	0	0	0	1

PB - Santovenia. T - 2:48. A - 14,321.

All-Tournament Team
Kevin Bernier, Maine, 1b
Jim Thomas, Wichita St., 2b
Phil Lane, Miami (Fla.), 3b
Spike Owen, Texas, ss
Loren Hibbs, Wichita St., of
Tim Gaskell, Wichita St, of
Mike Brumley, Texas, ss
Nelson Santovenia, Miami (Fla.), c
Russ Morman, Wichita St., of
Bryan Oelkers, Wichita St., p
Dan Smith, Miami (Fla.), p

1983
June 3, 1983

Texas	ab	r	h	rbi	Alabama	ab	r	h	rbi
Bates, 2b	5	0	1	0	Elbin, 3b	3	0	0	1
Brumley, ss	5	1	3	0	McClendon, dh	4	0	1	0
Killingsworth, dh	4	2	2	1	Magadan, 1b	4	1	2	0
Tolentino, 1b	5	1	2	1	Skates, lf	4	0	0	0
Hearron, c	3	0	0	0	Stallings, cf	4	0	2	1
Labay, rf	3	0	1	1	Velleggia, c	4	0	0	0
Sutton, lf	3	0	0	1	Lake, 2b	4	0	0	0
Trent, cf	3	0	0	0	Smithney, rf	3	0	2	0

All-Tournament Team
Dave Magadan, Alabama, 1b
Bill Bates, Texas, 2b
Chris Sabo, Michigan, 3b
Mike Brumley, Texas, ss
Barry Bonds,

The College World Series Record Book

Burrows, 3b	3	0	1	0	Shipley, ss	3	1	0	0
Totals	34	4	10	4	Totals	33	3	7	3

Texas   000 002 200 - 4
Alabama   001 010 001 - 3

Game winning RBI - Killingsworth. E - Hearron. LOB - Texas 9; Alabama 4. DP - Alabama 1. 2B - Burrows, Magadan. 3B - Killingsworth. HR - Smithney (5). SB - Trent (14). S - Sutton. SF - Elbin.

Texas			ER	H	R	ER	BB	SO
Clemens (W, 13-5)			9	7	3	3	0	9
Alabama								
Browne (L, 11-2)			7.2	8	4	4	3	8
Brouchle			1.1	2	0	0	0	0

HBP - Trent by Browne, Hearron by Browne. WP - Clemens 2. T-2:20. A -14,957.

1984
June 1, 1984

Texas	ab	r	h	rbi	Cal Fullerton	ab	r	h	rbi
Westbrooks, cf	3	1	1	0	Thomas, cf	3	0	0	0
Hodo, lf	1	0	1	0	Mota, 2b	3	0	0	0
Bates, 2b	2	0	0	0	Fishel, lf	3	0	1	0
Richards, 1b	4	0	1	1	Caffrey, c	3	1	1	0
Denny, 3b	4	0	0	0	Bryant, rf	3	2	1	1
Loy, c	4	0	0	0	Bates, 1b	4	0	1	1
Cook, rf	4	0	0	0	Sarkission, dh	2	0	0	1
Labay, dh	2	0	0	0	Turner, ss	3	0	1	0
Wrznski, cf	3	0	0	0	Larker, 3b	3	0	0	0
Doughty, ss	2	0	0	0					
Totals	29	1	3	1	Totals	27	3	5	3

Texas   100 000 000 - 1
Cal State Fullerton 010 200 00x - 3

Game winning RBI - Bryant. E - Mota, Doughty. DP - Fullerton 1. LOB - Texas 5, Fullerton 7. 2B - Hodo. 3B - Bryant. SB - Bryant (15), Fishel (28). S - Moto, Bates, Sarkission. SF - Sarkission.

Texas	IP	H	R	ER	BB	SO
Swindell (L, 14-2)	4.1	3	3	3	2	3
Boudreaux	3.2	2	0	0	1	3
Cal State Fullerton						
Delzer (W, 8-2)	7	2	1	1	3	7
Wright (S, 22)	2	1	0	0	0	1

HBP - Swindell (Bryant). T 0 2:24. A - 13,487.

1985
June 11, 1985

Miami (Fla.)	ab	r	h	rbi	Texas	ab	r	h	rbi
James, rf	5	1	2	0	Kerlin, ss	4	2	1	0
Fiore, lf	4	3	3	1	Bates, 2b	3	1	1	0
Leake, 3b	3	1	0	0	Cook, rf	4	1	1	1
Ellena, dh	5	2	4	1	Denny, lf	4	0	0	1
Rowland, 2b	4	1	2	1	Hodo, dh	4	1	2	0
DeBold, ss	3	1	1	0	Johnson, 3b	4	1	3	1
Nelson, ss	0	0	0	0	Richards, 1b	4	0	0	0

Arizona State, of
Dale Sklar,
Michigan, of
Tim Knapp,
Oklahoma St., of
Jeff Hearron,
Texas, c
Pete Incaviglia,
Oklahoma St., dh
Calvin Schiraldi,
Texas, p
Tim Meacham,
Alabama, p

All-Tournament Team
Rusty Richards, Texas, 1b
Randy Whisler, Oklahoma St., 2b
Blaine Larker, (tie) Cal St. Ful. 3b
Scott Raziano, (tie) New Orleans, 3b
Gary Green, Oklahoma St., ss
John Fishel, Cal St. Ful., of
Oddibe McDowell, Arizona State, of
Barry Bonds, Arizona State, of
Bob Caffrey, Cal St. Ful., c
Pete Incaviglia, Oklahoma St., dh
Greg Swindell, Texas, p
Eddie Delzer, Cal St. Ful., p

All-Tournament Team
Will Clark, Miss. St., 1b
Bill Bates, Texas, 2b
Jeff King, Arkansas, 3b
Frank Davis, Miss. St., ss
Dennis Cook,

39

Hart, 1b	4	1	1	1	Wrzesinski, cf	3	0	1	1
Sells, c	3	0	0	1	Byers, c	0	0	0	0
Richardi, cf	5	0	1	1	Bensch, ph	1	0	1	0
					Anderson, c	0	0	0	0
					Oertil, c	2	0	0	0
					Vanderkamp, cf	2	0	1	0
Totals	34	10	14	6	Totals	35	6	11	5

Game-winning RBI-Rowland. E-Kerlin, Bates, Cook, Johnson, Richards. DP-Texas 2. LOB-Miami 4, Texas 9. 2B-Richardi, Fiore, Johnson, Wrzesinski, Bates. 3B-James, Hodo. SB-Fiore, Rowland. S-DeBold. SF-Richardi, Denny.

Miami	IP	H	R	ER	BB	SO
Sheary (W, 7-4)	6.2	8	6	6	4	6
Raether	2.1	3	0	0	0	4
Texas						
Ruffin (L, 13-3)	2.1	6	4	3	1	1
Poehl	6.2	8	6	2	3	2

PB,-,Oerti 2, Solis. WP,-,Sheary. T,-,2:41. A,-,9,830.

1986

June 9, 1986

Florida State	ab	r	h	rbi	Arizona	ab	r	h	rbi
Marzan, 1b	4	0	1	0	Hinzo, 2b	4	2	1	0
Sorrento, rf	4	0	0	0	Hale, 3b	4	2	2	1
Alicea, 2b	4	1	1	0	Senne, lf	5	2	2	2
Figueroa, ss	4	1	2	1	Trafton, 1b	3	2	2	1
Mangham, cf	4	0	1	0	Strong, c	4	0	1	0
Toddeo, dh	2	0	1	0	Millay, rf	4	2	3	3
Zoeller, dh	1	0	0	0	Johnson, cf	4	0	0	0
Fulton, c	4	0	1	1	Alexander, dh	4	0	0	0
Blackwell, 3b	2	0	0	0	Rohde, ss	4	0	0	1
McClellan, ph	1	0	0	0					
Clayborne, lf	0	0	0	0					
Saxner ph	1	0	0	0					
Totals	31	2	7	2	Totals	36	10	11	8

Florida State 000 000 002 - 2
Arizona   000 114 31x - 10

E-Trafton, Mangham, Rohde, Blackwell, Hinzo. DP-Arizona 3. LOB-Florida State 6, Arizona 5. 2B-Figueroa, Millay, Hale, Senne, Mangham. 3B-Hale, Alicea. HR-Senne (11), Millay (9). SB-Toddeo (17), Rohde (19), Hinzo 3 (45). S-Clayborne.

Florida State	IP	H	R	ER	BB	SO
Loynd (L, 20-3)	5	3	3	1	1	6
Lewis	1.2	4	5	5	1	2
Porcelli	1.1	4	2	2	1	1
Arizona						
Alexander (W, 8-2)	9	7	2	2	2	5

Loynd pitched to 1 batter in the sixth. HBP-Clayborne by Alexander. WP-Loynd. T-2:44. A-12,659.

Texas, of
Dave Van Cleve,
Miss. St., of
Ralph Kraus,
Arkansas, of
Chris Magno,
Miami (Fla.), c
Greg Ellena,
Miami (Fla.), dh
Kevin Sheary,
Miami (Fla.), p
Greg Swindell,
Texas, p

All-Tournament Team
Todd Trafton,
Arkansas, 1b
Luis Alicea,
Florida State, 2b
Robin Ventura,
Oklahoma St., 3b
Bien Figueroa,
Florida State, ss
Mike Senne,
Arizona, of
Mike Flore,
Miami (Fla.), of
Paul Sorrento,
Florida State, of
Bill Reynolds,
Maine, c
Gary Alexander,
Arizona, dh
Richie Lewis,
Florida State, p
Gary Alexander,
Arizona, p

The College World Series Record Book

1987

June 7, 1987

Stanford	ab	r	h	rbi	Oklahoma St	ab	r	h	rbi
Amaro, lf	3	1	0	0	Blackmon, cf	3	1	1	0
Cook, cf	5	3	3	0	Ortiz, lf	5	1	2	0
Sprague, 3b	4	2	3	1	Ventura, 3b	5	0	4	1
P. Carey, rf	5	2	3	2	Ifland, dh	4	1	1	2
Wilmeyer, 1b	4	1	2	1	Barrouan, 1b	5	0	2	0
Esquer, ss	5	0	2	2	Fariss, ss	3	0	1	0
Rubbins, c	5	0	0	1	Smith, c	4	0	0	0
Machlolt, dh	4	0	2	0	Castillo, rf	3	1	1	0
F. Carey, 2b	4	0	0	0	Beanblossom, 2b	3	1	1	1
Totals	39	9	15	7	Totals	35	5	13	5

Stanford   200 040 003 - 9
Oklahoma St   001 210 001 - 5

Game-winning RBI - Sprague. E-Castillo, F. Carey. LOB - Stanford 8, Oklahoma State 11. DP - Stanford 4, Oklahoma State 2. 2B - Ventura 2, Cook, P. Carey 2, Wilmeyer. HR - Castilla (11), Beanblossom (31), Ifland (15). SB - Cook 2 (28), Esquer (16). SF-Sprague, Ifland.

	IP	H	R	ER	BB	SO
Stanford						
McDowell (W, 13-5)	7	12	4	3	4	7
Chitren (S, 13)	2	1	1	1	1	3
Oklahoma State						
Hape (L, 13-3)	5.1	11	6	6	2	3
Rockman	2.2	4	3	2	1	3
Long	1	0	0	0	1	1

McDowell pitched to two batters in the eighth. Rockman pitched to three batters in the ninth. HBP - Blackmon by McDowell, Blackmon by Chitren. WP - McDowell, Hope 2. PB - Smith. T - 3:04. A - 14,132.

All-Tournament Team
Jimmy Barragan, Oklahoma St., 1b
Brad Beanblossom, Oklahoma St., 2b
Scott Coolbaugh, Texas, 3b
David Esquer, Stanford, ss
Brian Cisarik, Texas, of
Jack Voigt, LSU, of
Paul Carey, Stanford, of
Adam Smith, Oklahoma St., c
Mark Machtolf, Stanford, dh
Pat Hope, Oklahoma St., p
Greg Patterson, LSU, p

1988

June 11, 1988

Arizona St	ab	r	h	rbi	Stanford	ab	r	h	rbi
Listach, ss	5	0	2	0	F. Corey, 2b	5	0	2	0
Manahan, pr	0	0	0	0	Paulsen, ss	5	0	2	1
Finn, 3b	4	1	1	0	Sprague, 3b	4	1	2	2
Higgins, 2b	4	1	2	0	P. Carey, rf	4	1	1	1
Willis, 1b	4	1	1	3	Robbins, c	3	1	0	0
Rumsey, rf	4	1	2	0	Wilmeyer, 1b	3	2	2	1
Peralta, dh	4	0	0	0	Johnson, lf	4	0	1	2
Spehr, c	4	0	1	0	Griffin, dh	4	1	1	1
Candaelari, lf	4	0	1	0	Eicher, cf	0	0	0	0
Burralo, cf	4	0	0	0	DeGraw, cf	4	1	2	0
Totals	37	4	10	3	Totals	34	9	13	8

Arizona State   000 100 030 - 4
Stanford   512 001 00x - 9

Game-winning RBI - Sprague. E - Robbins, Sprague, Listach. DP - Stanford 1. LOB - Arizona St 7, Stanford 7. 2B - Johnson, Higgins, Griffin, Wilmeyer. 3B - Spehr, Rumsey. HR - Sprague (22), Willis (7). SB - Finn (16), DeGraw (9). SF - P. Carey.

All-Tournament Team
Ron Witmeyer, Stanford, 1b
Mark Standiford, Wichita St., 2b
John Finn, Arizona State, 3b
Pat Listach, Arizona State, ss
Jim Osborn, Cal St. Ful., of
Dan Rumsey, Arizona State, of
Ricky Candelari, Arizona State, of
Doug Robbins, Stanford, c
Martin Peralta, Arizona State, dh

41

Arizona State	IP	H	R	ER	BB	SO
Kilgo (L, 12-3)	.1	4	5	5	1	0
Minor	.2	3	1	1	0	0
Ingram	7	6	3	3	1	8
Stanford						
Spencer (W, 7-2)	7	9	4	3	1	4
Chitren	2	1	0	0	0	1

Lee Plemel, Stanford, p
Rusty Kilgo, Arizona State, p

Minor pitched to 2 batters in the 2nd; Spencer pitched to 4 batters in the 8th. HBP-Sprague by Ingram. WP-Ingram 3. T-2:55. A-16,071.

1989

June 10, 1989

Texas	ab	r	h	rbi	Wichita State	ab	r	h	rbi
Jones cf	2	0	1	0	Audley cf	3	0	0	0
Tollison 2b	4	0	1	0	Forbes 2b	3	1	0	0
Bryant dh-p	4	1	1	0	McDonald lf-1b	4	0	0	0
Butcher lf	4	1	1	0	Wedge c	3	0	0	0
Newkirk 3b	3	1	1	0	Winslow 1b	2	0	1	1
Lowery 1b	3	0	1	1	Wilson lf	2	1	1	0
Shults rf	3	0	0	1	Meares ss	3	1	1	2
Bethea ss	4	0	0	0	Dreifort rf	4	0	1	0
Prather c	3	0	0	0	Jones 3b	4	1	1	0
Pate ph	1	0	0	0	Wentworth ph	4	1	2	0
Totals	31	3	6	2	Totals	32	5	7	3

Texas   000 201 000 - 3
Wichita State   120 020 00x - 5

E-Newkirk 2, Tollison, Dreifort, Winslow, Bethea. DP-Wichita State 1. LOB-Texas 6, Wichita State 8. HR-Meares (9). S-Audley. SF-Lowery.

Texas	IP	H	R	ER	BB	SO
Bryant (L 1-1)	.2	1	1	1	4	0
Dare	7.1	6	4	2	0	7
Wichita State						
Brummett (W, 18-2)	9	6	3	1	4	6

PB-Wedge. Umpires-Williams, Steiner, Jones, Graham, Ravan, Roberts. T-2:59. A-13,701.

All-Tournament Team

David Lowery, Texas, 1b
Rocky Rau, Florida State, 2b
Craig Newkirk, Texas, 3b
Pat Meares, Wichita St., ss
Todd Dreifort, Wichita St., of
Jim Audley, Wichita St., of
Arthur Butcher, Texas, of
Eric Wedge, Wichita St., c
Scott Bryant, Texas, dh
Jim Newlin, Wichita St., p
Greg Brummett, Wichita St., p

1990

June 9, 1990

Georgia	ab	r	h	rbi	Oklahoma St.	ab	r	h	rbi
Smith cf	4	0	1	0	Simons 2b	3	1	2	0
Cooper 3b	3	1	1	1	Carlsen 3b	3	0	0	0
Showalter ss	4	0	2	0	Beanblossom ss	3	0	1	0
Jester dh	2	0	0	0	Daniel c	3	0	0	1
Chick rf	3	0	0	1	Burnitz rf	3	0	0	0
Radziewicz 1b	4	0	0	0	Kelly dh	4	0	2	0
Suplee lf	3	0	0	0	Dailey lf	4	0	0	0
Childers c	4	1	2	0	Perez cf	3	0	0	0
Alfonso 2b	4	0	0	0	Cervantes 1b	0	0	0	0
					Walbergh ph-1b	2	0	0	0
Totals	31	2	5	2	Totals	28	1	5	1

Georgia   000 110 000 - 2

All-Tournament Team

Doug Radziewicz, Georgia, 1b
Troy Paulsen, Stanford, 2b
Bobby Carlsen, Oklahoma St., 3b
Brad Beanblossom, Oklahoma St., ss
Tim Clark, LSU, of
Jeff Hammonds, Stanford, of
Jason Rychlick,

The College World Series Record Book

Oklahoma State 000 001 000 - 1
E-Showalter, Moody. DP-Georgia 3, Oklahoma St. 1. LOB-Georgia 7, Oklahoma St 6. 2B-Smith, Kelly. SH-Carlesen. SF-Chick, Daniel.

Georgia	IP	H	R	ER	BB	SO
Payne (W)	6	4	1	1	3	6
Fleming (S)	3	1	0	0	1	4
Oklahoma St.						
Burbank (L)	6.2	6	2	2	1	2
Moody	2.1	0	0	0	2	4

HBP-Jester (by Burbank). T-2:53. A-16,482.

Citadel, of
Michael Daniel, Oklahoma St., c
Lyle Mouton, LSU, dh
Dave Fleming, Georgia, p
Mike Rebhan, Georgia, p

1991

May 8, 1991

LSU	ab	r	h	rbi	Wichita State	ab	r	h	rbi
Johnson, 2b	4	1	1	0	Hall, 2b	3	1	2	0
Rios, cf	3	3	2	2	Wimmer, ss	4	0	1	0
Mouton, rf	4	2	0	0	Audley, cf	3	1	0	1
Cordani, lf	4	0	1	3	Mirabelli, c	3	0	0	0
Hymel, c	3	0	1	0	T. Dreifort, rf	3	0	1	1
Garrity, dh	4	0	2	1	White, 1b	4	0	0	0
Tallachea, 1b	3	0	0	0	Tilma, lf	3	1	1	1
C. Moock, 3b	3	0	0	0	Jones, 3b	3	0	0	0
Sheets, ss	3	0	1	0	McCloughan, dh	1	0	0	0
					D. Dreifort, dh	3	0	0	0
Totals	31	6	8	6	Totals	30	3	5	3

Louisiana State 220 200 000 - 6
Wichita State   100 100 010 - 3
E-Green. DP-LSU 1, Wichita State 3. LOB-LSU 7, Wichita State 5. 2B-Rios. 3B-Cordani. HR-Rios, Tilma.

LSU	IP	H	R	ER	BB	SO
Ogea (W, 14-5)	7	4	3	2	4	3
Greene (S, 14)	2	1	0	0	0	2
Wichita State						
Green (L, 11-2)	3	5	4	4	3	3
D. Driefort	4.1	3	2	2	2	1
Bluma	1.2	0	0	0	0	2

All-Tournament Team
John Tellechea, LSU, 1b
Mike McCafferty, Creighton, 2b
Jason Giambi, Long Beach St., 3b
Kevin Polcovich, Florida, ss
Lyle Mouton, LSU, of
Jim Audley, Wichita St., of
Steve Hinton, Creighton, of
Gary Hymel, LSU, c
Mario Linares, Florida, dh
Kennie Steenstra, Wichita St., p
Chad Ogea, LSU, p

1992

June 6, 1992

Pepperdine	ab	r	h	rbi	Fullerton	ab	r	h	rbi
Rodriguez, 2b	3	1	0	0	Carr, rf	3	0	1	0
McElreath, rf	4	0	1	0	Powell, cf	2	1	0	0
Melendez, 1b	4	0	1	0	Nevin, 3b	3	0	1	0
Main, dh	4	1	2	1	Moler, c-1b	2	0	0	1
Wasikowski, 3b	4	0	1	1	Banks, lf	3	0	0	0
Lovell, 3b	0	0	0	0	Sisco, 2b	4	0	0	0
Vollmer, c	4	0	2	0	Fairbrother, dh	4	0	1	0
Sheff, cf	3	0	0	0	Olsen, 1b	2	0	1	0
Dell' Amico, lf	4	0	0	0	Hemphill, c	4	0	0	0
Ekdal, ss	3	1	1	1	Rodriquez, ss	4	1	0	0

All-Tournament Team
Dan Melendez, Pepperdine, 1b
Steve Rodriguez, Pepperdine, 2b
Phil Nevin, Cal St. Fullerton, 3b
Nate Rodriquez, Cal St. Fullerton, ss
Byron Matthews, Oklahoma, of
Chris Powell, Cal St. Fullerton, of

The College World Series Record Book

Totals	33	3	8	3

Totals	27	2	4	1

Pepperdine   200 010 000 - 3
Cal State Fullerton 000 100 010 - 2
DP - Pepperdine 1. LOB - Pepperdine 5, Fullerton 4. 2B - Main (16), Melendez (15). HR - Ekdal (1). SB - Rodriquez (35). S - Shell; C. Powell. SF - Maier.

Pepperdine	IP	H	R	ER	BB	SO
Ahearne (W, 15-2)	6.2	3	1	0	3	3
Wallace	.1	1	0	0	0	1
Montgomery (S, 9)	2	0	1	1	1	0
Fullerton						
Naulty (L, 13-4)	1	3	2	2	1	0
Chavez	5.2	3	1	1	0	2
Dembisky	2.1	2	0	0	0	1

HBP - Rodriquez (by Montgomery), Carr (by Montogmery). PB - Vollmer. A - 2.56. A - 17,962.

Johnathen Smith, Miami, of
Scott Vollmer, Pepperdine, c
Brooks Kieschnick, Texas, dh
Patrick Ahearne, Pepperdine, p
James Popoff, Cal St. Fullerton, p

1993
June 12, 1993

Wichita State	ab	r	h	rbi	LSU	ab	r	h	rbi
Hall, rf	5	0	0	0	Williams, 3b	3	1	1	1
Adams, ss	4	0	1	0	Rios, cf	3	0	1	4
Taylor, cf	3	0	0	0	Johnson, ss	3	1	1	0
Smith, 1b	4	0	0	0	Walker, 2b	4	1	2	3
Driefort, dh-p	3	0	1	0	Berrios, rf	4	0	2	0
J. Jackson, 2b	4	0	0	0	Neal, dh	4	1	1	0
Blake, 3b	3	0	0	0	Greely, lf	2	2	1	0
Tilma, lf	3	0	1	0	Huffman, lf	0	0	0	0
McCollough, c	2	0	0	0	Antonini, c	2	1	0	0
Wheeler, c	0	0	0	0	F. Jackson, 1b	3	1	1	0
Mills, ph	1	0	0	0					
Totals	32	0	3	0	Totals	28	8	10	8

Wichita State   000 000 000 - 0
Louisiana State 232 000 01x - 8
E - Greely (5), K. Jackson (14). DP - Wichita State 2. LOB - Wichita State 10, Louisiana State 7. 2B - K. Jackson (18). HR - Walker (22). SB - Greely (3), Johnson (19). SH - K. Jackson, Williams. SF - Rios 2.

Wichita State	IP	H	R	ER	BB	SO
Wyckoff (L, 5-3)	1.1	3	5	5	3	0
Dreifort	1.2	3	2	2	2	2
Baird	5	3	1	1	1	4
Louisiana State						
Laxton (W, 12-1)	9	3	0	0	5	16

All-Tournament Team
Hunter Triplett, Oklahoma St., 1b
Todd Walker, LSU, 2b
Casey Blake, Wichita State, 3b
Jason Adams, Wichita State, ss
Jim Greely, LSU, of
Jason Heath, Oklahoma St., ss
Amanda Rios, LSU, of
Adrian Antonini, LSU, c
Jeff Liefer, Long Beach St., dh
Brett Laxton, LSU, p
Mike Sirotka, LSU, p

1994
June 11, 1994

Georgia Tech	ab	r	h	rbi	Oklahoma	ab	r	h	rbi
Garciaparra ss	5	1	2	1	Thomas lf	5	3	3	1
McIntyre 2b	5	0	0	0	Hansen lf	0	0	0	0
Payton cf	5	0	2	0	Traylor rf	4	3	3	1
Varitek c	3	2	2	1	Guiterrez 2b	4	1	2	3

All-Tournament Team
Ryan Minor, Oklahoma, 1b
Rick Gutierrez, Oklahoma, 2b
Antone Williamson, Arizona State, 3b

The College World Series Record Book

	ab	r	h	rbi		ab	r	h	rbi
Hensley, 1b	4	1	1	1	D. Minor, dh	4	1	2	2
Byers, 2b	1	0	0	0	Bradshaw, ph	0	0	0	0
Barr, ph	0	0	0	0	Hills, ss	4	1	2	2
Lincoln, pr	0	1	0	0	Glass, cf	5	2	2	1
Easterling, lf	0	0	0	0	Mariani, 1b	3	0	2	2
Sorrow, dh	2	0	1	2	R. Minor, 3b	4	1	0	0
Milan, ph	1	0	1	0	Soto, ph	1	0	0	0
Smith, rf	4	0	1	1	Flores, c	5	1	1	0
Saier, cf	1	0	0	0					
Fitter, ph	1	0	0	0					
Totals	34	5	10	5	Totals	39	13	16	13

George Tech   011 002 010 - 5
Oklahoma   200 504 30x - 13

E - Hensley 2, Saier, Varitek. DP - Georgia Tech 3, Oklahoma 1. LOB - Georgia Tech 6, Oklahoma 8. 2B - Payton, Sorrow. Hills. 3B - Traylor. HR - Garciaparra, Varitek, D. Minor, Glass. SB-Garciaparra, Morloni.

Georgia Tech	IP	H	R	ER	BB	SO
Gogolin (L, 12-3)	3.1	7	7	3	3	0
Myers	2.2	5	4	4	0	3
McGill	1	4	2	2	1	0
Cason	1	0	0	0	1	1
Oklahoma						
Lovingier	2	3	2	2	2	2
Synder	1	1	0	0	1	0
Walton (W, 7-3)	2.1	2	2	2	2	1
Buckles (S, 14)	3.2	4	1	1	1	2

HBP - by Myers (Hills). WP - McGill. U - Runchey, Pedersen, Nelson, Magnusson. T - 2:50. A - 21,602.

1995
June 10, 1995

Southern Cal	ab	r	h	rbi	Cal St. Ful.	ab	r	h	rbi
Dawkins, cf	4	1	1	1	Miranda, lf	4	2	2	2
Cruz, dh	3	0	0	0	Ankrum, dh	4	2	2	1
Ponchak, ph	1	0	0	0	Chatham, cf	0	0	0	0
Alvarez, ss	4	0	0	0	Kotsay, cf-p	4	2	2	5
Jenkins, rf	4	2	2	1	Giambi, rf	5	0	2	0
Jones, lf	3	1	1	0	Loyd, c	5	0	1	0
Moeller, c	4	0	1	0	Fraser, 2b	4	1	1	0
Walbridge, 1b	3	0	0	0	Olsen, 1b	4	2	1	0
Carson, ph	1	0	1	0	Jones, ss	3	1	0	0
Montoya, pr	0	0	0	0	Martinez, 3b	3	1	1	3
Diaz, 3b	4	1	2	3					
Rachels, 2b	3	0	0	0					
Totals	34	5	8	5	Totals	36	11	12	11

Southern Cal   032 000 000 - 5
Cal St. Fullerton 340 000 40x - 11

E - Alvarez, Etherton, Walbridge, Olsen. DP - Cal St. Fullerton 1. LOB - Southern Cal 3, Cal St. Fullerton 8. 2B - Diaz, Jenkins. HR - Dawkins, Diaz, Jenkins, Kotsay, Martinez, Miranda. SH - Jacque Jones, Ankrum, Fraser, Jack Jones, Martinez.

Southern Cal	IP	H	R	ER	BB	SO

Nomar Garciaparra, Georgia Tech, ss
Mark Kotsay, Cal St. Fullerton, of
Darvin Traylor, Oklahoma, of
Chip Glass, Oklahoma, of
Jason Varitek, Georgia Tech, c
Todd Walker, LSU, dh
Mark Redman, Oklahoma, p
Brad Rigby, Georgia Tech, p

Oklahoma's Kevin Lovinger went onto the pros.

All-Tournament Team

Doug Mientkiewicz, Florida State, 1b
Wes Rachels, Southern Cal., 2b
Tony Martinez, Cal St. Fullerton, 3b
Alex Cora, Miami (Fla.), ss
J.D. Drew, Florida State, of
Goeff Jenkins, Southern Cal., of
Mark Kotsay, Cal St. Fullerton, of
Brian Loyd, Cal St. Fullerton, c
Scott Schroeffel, Tennessee, dh
Randy Flores, Southern Cal., p

The College World Series Record Book

Cooper (L)	3.1	7	7	3	1	0
Etherton	3.1	3	4	0	2	3
Krawczyk	1.1	2	0	0	0	0
Cal St. Fullerton						
Silva (W)	7.1	6	5	2	0	5
Kotsay	1.2	2	0	0	0	2

WP - Etherton. T - 3:01. A - 22,027.

Ted Silva, Cal St. Fullerton, p

1996
June 8, 1996

Miami (Fla.)	ab	r	h	rbi	LSU	ab	r	h	rbi
Grimmett cf	3	2	0	0	Williams ss	4	0	1	0
Gomez 2b	5	1	3	0	Koerner cf	4	1	2	2
Burrell dh	4	1	1	1	Dunn 3b	4	1	2	2
Rivero rf-lf	3	1	1	1	Furniss 1b	4	0	2	1
DeCelle lf	4	0	2	3	Cooley lf	5	0	1	0
Moore rf	0	0	0	0	Wilson dh	5	1	1	0
Marcinczyk 1b	5	2	2	0	Bowles rf	5	0	2	0
Cora ss	5	0	3	3	Lanier c	3	2	1	0
Saggese dh	5	0	2	0	Morris 2b	4	4	3	2
Gargiulo c	3	1	0	0					
Totals	37	8	14	8	Totals	38	9	15	7

Miami (Fla.)   200 032 001 - 8
LSU   003 000 222 - 9

E - Burrell, Rivera, Dunn, Furniss. LOB - Miami 9, LSU 10. 2B - Marcinczyk, Cora, Saggese, Wilson, Bowles, Morris. 3B - Cora. HR - Morris. SB - Gomez, Koerner, Lanier, CS - Koerner. SH - Grimmett, Morris. SF - Burrell, Rivero, DeCelle, Koerner, Dunn.

Miami	IP	H	R	ER	BB	SO
Arteaga	6.2	10	5	3	2	7
Morrison (L)	2	5	4	4	2	2
LSU						
Shipp	5.2	11	7	5	3	3
Coogan (W)	3.1	3	1	1	0	1

WP - Morrison. T - 3:19. A - 23,905.

All-Tournament Team
Chris Moller, Alabama, 1b
Rudy Gomez, Miami (Fla.), 2b
Pat Burrell, Miami (Fla.), 3b
Alex Cora, Miami (Fla.), ss
Justin Bowles, LSU, of
Michael DeCelle, Miami (Fla.), of
Brad Wilkerson, Florida, of
Tim Lanier, LSU, c
Chuck Hazzard, Florida, dh
J.D. Arteaga, Miami (Fla.), p
Eddie Yarnall, LSU, p

1997
June 11, 1997

Alabama	ab	r	h	rbi	LSU	ab	r	h	rbi
Tidwell cf	5	2	2	0	Higgins dh	4	1	2	3
Caruso 2b	4	1	3	4	Barbier 2b	5	1	1	0
Phillips 3b	5	0	1	0	Larson ss	6	1	2	3
Mohr rf	4	0	1	0	Furniss 1b	5	1	3	0
Keller lf	4	1	0	0	Koerner cf	6	2	2	1
Frick c	5	1	1	0	McClure 3b	3	1	0	0
Tucker 1b	4	0	1	2	Bernhardt rf	4	3	3	3
Peer dh	4	1	1	0	Witten rf	0	0	0	0
Duncan ss	4	0	1	0	Davis lf	4	1	1	3
					Earnhart c	2	0	0	0
					Horton c	1	2	1	0
Totals	39	6	11	6	Totals	40	13	15	13

All-Tournament Team
Eddie Furniss, LSU, 1b
Joe Caruso, Alabama, 2b
Andy Phillips, Alabama, 3b
Brandon Larson, LSU, ss
Mike Koerner, LSU, of
Tom Bernhardt, LSU, of
G.W. Keller, Alabama, of
Matt Frick, Alabama, c

The College World Series Record Book

Alabama	002	200	020 - 6	
Louisiana State	630	002	11x - 13	

E - Caruso, Duncan, Henderson, McClure. DP - Alabama 1, LSU 1. LOB - Alabama 9, LSU 13. 2B - Caruso, Phillips, Tucker, Peer, Bernhardt, Davis. HR - Caruso, Higgins, Bernhardt. SB - Caruso

Alabama	IP	H	R	ER	BB	SO
Daniel (L, 5-1)	.2	5	5	4	0	0
Kingrey	3.2	5	4	0	6	4
Henderson	2.1	4	3	2	1	4
Hurst	1.1	1	1	1	2	2
LSU						
Coogan (W, 12-3)	4.1	6	4	4	1	8
Thompson	4.2	5	2	2	1	7

HBP - by Coogan (Keller), by Henderson (McClure). T - 3:15. A - 24,401. U - Davis, Garman, Magnusson, Hernandez.

Mark Peer, Alabama, dh
Jeff Austin, Stanford, p
Jarrod Kingrey, Alabama, p

1998

June 6, 1998

Southern Cal	ab	h	r	rbi	Arizona State	ab	h	r	rbi
Rachels, 2b	7	3	5	7	Bloomquist, 2b	6	0	1	0
Hanoian, lf	2	1	0	0	Arguelles, cf	5	2	1	2
Perry, pr-cf	1	0	1	0	Moreno, rf	6	2	2	1
Gorr, 1b	5	3	2	5	Beinbrink, 3b	2	2	1	3
Munson, c	6	1	2	0	Phelps, 1b	4	1	2	2
Ensberg, 3b	4	3	2	1	Delucchi, lf	5	1	1	1
Ticehurst, rf	5	2	1	2	Myers, dh	5	3	4	1
Lane, dh-p	6	2	3	4	Halvonson, c	5	3	2	0
Freitas, cf-lf	6	3	5	1	Collins, ss	3	1	1	4
DePippo, pr-lf	0	0	0	0					
Davidson, ss	4	3	2	0					
Totals	46	21	23	20	Totals	41	14	16	14

Southern Cal	351	002	325 - 21	
Arizona State	050	300	510 - 14	

E - Davidson. DP - Arizona State 2. LOB - USC 7, Arizona State 8. 2B - Rachels, Ensberg, Lane, Freitas, Moreno. HR - Rachels, Gorr 2, Ticehurst, Lane, beinbrink, Phelps, Myers, Collins. SB - Ensberg, Freitas, Davidson, Moreno. SH - Hanoian, Collins 2. SF - Gorr, Beinbrink.

	IP	H	R	ER	BB	SO
Southern Cal						
Currier	1.1	5	5	5	1	3
Lane (W, 9-2)	2.1	4	3	0	2	1
Immel	3	4	4	4	2	1
Weibling	0.2	3	2	2	0	1
Krawczyk	1.2	0	0	0	0	1
Arizona State						
Mills (L, 8-4)	1	6	6	6	1	1
Kramer	5	6	5	5	3	1
Pennington	1.1	5	5	5	3	1
Lowery	1	4	4	4	2	0
Crumpton	.2	2	1	1	0	0

PB - Halvorsen 2. HBP - by Kramer (Ensberg). T-3:59. A - 24,456.

All-Tournament Team
Robb Gorr, Southern Cal, 1b
Wes Rachels, Southern Cal, 2b
Andrew Beinbrink, Arizona St., 3b
Michael Collins, Arizona St., of
Rudy Arguellas, Arizona St., of
Cedrick Harris, LSU, of
Brad Ticehurst, Southern Cal, of
Eric Munson, Southern Cal, c
Jason Lane, Southern Cal, dh
Alex Santos, Miami, p
Jack Krawczyk, Southern Cal, p

The College World Series Record Book

1999
June 11, 1999

Florida State	ab	r	h	rbi	Miami (Fla.)	ab	r	h	rbi
Griffin, lf	2	0	1	2	Hill, ss	2	1	2	0
McDougall, 2b	5	0	1	0	Seever, cf	4	0	1	1
Diaz, rf	4	1	2	0	Crespo, rf	2	1	0	0
Scott, dh	4	2	1	1	Esquivel, 3b	3	1	1	0
Klosterman, c	5	0	0	0	Brown, 1b	4	1	2	4
Cash, 3b	4	0	1	1	Rodriguez, lf	3	0	0	0
Smith, cf	4	0	0	0	Nettles, dh	3	1	1	0
Groves, ss	2	1	0	0	Lovelady, c	4	0	0	0
Barthelemy, 1b	4	1	1	0	Clute, 2b	3	1	1	1
Totals	34	5	7	4	Totals	28	6	8	6

Florida State 011 000 210 - 5
Miami (Fla.)   010 050 00x - 6

E-Whidden, Hill, Crespo. DP-Florida St. 10; Miami 5. 2B-Brown. 3B-Barthelemy. HR-Scott, Brown. SB-Hill. SH-Crespo. SF-Griffin.

Florida State	IP	H	R	ER	BB	SO
Varnes (L, 11-2)	6	8	6	6	4	1
Whidden	2	0	0	0	2	2
Miami						
Santos (W, 13-3)	5	4	2	1	5	4
Vazquez	2	2	2	2	2	2
Neu (S)	2	1	1	1	0	2

WP - Varnes, Vazquez. U - Rich Fetchiet, Dan Pedersen, Bill Davis, Randy Bruns, Tim Norman, Ken Couch. T - 2:50. A - 23,563.

All-Tournament Team
John Gall, Stanford, 1b
Marshall McDougall, Florida St., 2b
Lale Esquivel, Miami (Fla.), 3b
Bobby Hill, Miami (Fla.), ss
Matt Diaz, Florida State, of
G.W. Keller, Alabama, of
Manny Crespo, Miami (Fla.), of
Jeremiah Klosterman, Florida State, c
Sam Scott, Florida State, dh

2000
June 17, 2000

Stanford	ab	r	h	rbi	LSU	ab	r	h	rbi
Thompson, 1b	5	1	3	4	Theriot, ss	5	1	1	0
Bruntlett, ss	4	0	1	0	Fontenot, 2b	3	0	1	0
Muth, cf	4	0	0	0	Cresse, c	3	0	1	1
Gall, 3b	5	0	2	1	Hawpe, 1b	3	0	0	0
Borchard, rf	4	0	0	0	Barbier, 3b	3	1	1	1
O'Riordan, 2b	5	1	2	0	Pontiff, dh	3	2	1	0
Topham, lf	5	1	2	0	Harris, cf	4	1	1	1
VanZandt, dh	4	0	1	0	Witten, lf	3	1	2	2
Alvarado, c	3	2	2	0	Wright, rf	3	0	0	0
Totals	39	5	13	5	Totals	30	6	8	6

```
              R  H  E
Stanford  000 401 000 - 5  13  0
LSU       020 000 031 - 6   8  0
```

DP - Stanford, 1. LOB - Stanford 11, LSU 9. 2B - Thompson, VanZandt, Fontenot, Pontiff. HR - Thompson, Barbier, Witten. SB - Bruntlett. CS - O'Riordan. SH - Wright.

Stanford	IP	H	R	ER	BB	SO
Young	4	4	2	2	1	2
Wayne (LP)	4	4	4	4	3	7
LSU						
Tallet	5	11	5	5	1	4

All-Tournament Team
Craig Thompson, Stanford, 1b
Mike Fontenot, LSU, 2b
Blair Barbier, LSU, 3b
Ryan Theriot, LSU, ss
Steven Feehan, La.-Lafayette, of
Edmund Muth, Stanford, of
Joe Borchard, Stanford, of
Beau Craig, Southern Cal., c
Brad Hawpe, LSU, dh
Jon McDonald, Florida State, p
Trey Hodges, LSU, p

The College World Series Record Book

Hodges (WP) 4 2 0 0 1 4
BK - Hodges. HBP - Cresse (by Young), Alvarado (by Tallet), Borchard (by Hodges), Barbier (by Wayne) Fontenot (by Wayne). T - 3.42. A - 24,282. U - Scott Graham, Al Davis, Joe Burleson, Dan Mascorro, Tony Maners, David Wiley.

2001
June 16, 2001

Stanford	ab	r	h	rbi	Miami (Fla.)	ab	r	h	rbi
O'Riordan, 2b	4	0	0	0	Jimerson, cf	5	0	1	0
Fuld, cf	3	0	1	0	M. Rodriguez, lf	2	1	0	1
Garko, c	3	0	2	0	J. Rodriguez, ss	4	3	2	0
Quentin, rf	4	0	1	0	Matienzo, dh	2	3	2	1
Ash, dh	2	0	0	0	Nettles, ph	1	0	0	0
Garza, ph	1	0	0	0	Howard, 3b	4	3	2	1
Topham, 3b-ss	3	0	0	0	Mannix, rf	3	0	2	3
Swope, ph	1	0	0	0	Burt, rf	1	0	1	0
Hall, lf-eb	3	0	0	0	Brown, 1b	5	1	2	5
Naatjes, ph	1	0	0	0	Clute, 2b	4	1	1	0
Dragicevich, ss	1	0	1	0	Lovelady, c	4	0	0	0
Cooper, ph-lf	2	0	0	0					
VanZandt, 1b	2	1	0	0					
Totals	30	1	5	1	Totals	35	12	13	11

```
                              R   H   E
Stanford      000 001 000  -  1   5   2
Miami (Fla.)  004 052 01x  - 12  13   0
```

E - Quentin, Dragicevich. DP - Miami (Fla.) 2. LOB - Stanford 6, Miami (Fla.) 7. 2B - Garko, J. Rodriguez, Matienzo, Mannix, Brown. HR - Brown. SH - Mannix. SF - M. Rodriquez.

Stanford	IP	H	R	ER	BB	SO
Gosling (L, 7-3)	4.0	7	7	7	3	2
Bruksch	0.1	2	2	1	0	0
Wodnicki	0.2	1	2	2	2	0
Hudgins	1.0	1	0	0	0	0
McCally	1.0	0	0	0	0	1
Wilcox	1.0	2	1	0	0	1
Miami	IP	H	R	ER	BB	SO
Farmer (W, 15-2)	5.2	4	1	1	2	3
DeBold	2.1	1	0	0	2	2
Prendes	1.0	0	0	0	0	0

HBP - M. Rodriquez (by Gosling). WP - Farmer. U - Walsh, Henderson, Eldridge, Rodriquez. T - 3:09. A- 24,070.

All-Tournament Team
Kevin Brown, Miami (Fla.), 1b
David Bacani, Cal St. Fullerton, 2b
Kris Bennett, Tennessee, 3b
Chris Burke, Tennessee, ss
Jeff Christensen, Tennessee, of
Sam Fuld, Stanford, of
Charlton Jimerson, Miami (Fla.), of
Ryan Garko, Stanford, c
Danny Matienzo, Miami (Fla.), dh
Jeff Bruksch, Stanford, p
Tom Farmer, Miami (Fla.), p

2002
June 22, 2002

South Carolina	ab	r	h	rbi	Texas	ab	r	h	rbi
Meyer, ss	4	1	1	0	Moss, 2b	5	1	2	0
Harris, cf	5	0	2	2	Quintanilla, 3b	5	2	4	1
Peters, 1b	4	1	1	1	Majewski, rf	4	3	2	2
Thomas, rf	5	0	2	1	Rosenberg, rf	0	0	0	0
Dyson, dh	4	0	2	1	Ontiveros, 1b	4	2	1	0
Gonce, lf	2	0	0	0	Fahey, ss	3	2	2	3

All-Tournament Team
Michael Johnson, Clemson, 1b
Tim Moss, Texas, 2b
Omar Quintanilla, Texas, 3b
Victor Menocal, Georgia Tech, ss

The College World Series Record Book

Bell, lf	1	0	0	0	Hubele, c	2	0	0	2
Smith, ph	1	0	0	0	Carmichael, lf	4	1	1	3
Seaton, lf	0	0	0	0	Reininger, dh	3	1	0	0
Greenwood, ph	1	0	0	0	Hollimon, ph	1	0	0	0
Buscher, 3b	4	0	0	0	Napoleon, ph	4	0	1	0
Powell, c	4	2	2	0	Ferin pr/cf	0	0	0	0
Melillo, 2b	0	2	0	0	Simmons, p	0	0	0	0
Totals	35	6	10	5	Totals	35	12	13	11

South Carolina   110 000 220 - 6
Texas   310 031 04x - 12

E - Buscher, Powell, Melillo, Moss, Fahey. DP - Texas 2. LOB - SC 9, Texas 10. 2B - Peters, Dyson, Powell, Quintanilla 2, Majewski, Fahey, Napoleon. 3B - Majewski. HR - Carmichael. HBP - Melillo 2. SF - Dyson, Fahey, Hubele 2. SB - Fahey. U - Jim Garman, John Magnusson, Nick Zibelli, A.J. Lostaglio, Perry Costello, Kevin Daugherty. T - 3:19. A - 24.089.

Justin Harris, South Carolina, of
Sam Fuld, Stanford, of
Dustin Majewski, Texas, of
Steve Stanley, Notre Dame, dh
Landon Powell, South Carolina, c
Justin Simmons, Texas, p
Huston Street, Texas, p

South Carolina	**IP**	**H**	**R**	**ER**	**BB**	**SO**
Rawl (LP)	3.1	5	4	3	3	2
Spigner	1.0	2	3	2	1	0
Wesley	1.1	2	1	1	2	0
Campbell	1.1	3	4	4	1	1
Taylor	1.0	1	0	0	1	1
Texas	**IP**	**H**	**R**	**ER**	**BB**	**SO**
Simmons (WP)	6.2	8	4	3	2	4
Bomer	.2	1	2	1	1	1
Street (S)	1.2	1	0	0	1	1

Texas fans root for their Longhorns during action in the 2002 College World Series.

The College World Series Record Book

All-Time Won-Lost Record
(1947-2002)

Team (Years Participated)	Appearances	Won	Lost	Pct
Alabama (50-83-96-97-99)	5	11	10	.524
Arizona (54-55-56-58-59-60-63-66-70-76-79-80-85-86)	14	32	25	.561
Arizona St. (64-65-67-69-72-73-75-76-77-78-81-83-84-87-88-93-94-98)	18	55	30	.647
Arkansas (79-85-87-89)	4	7	8	.467
Auburn (67-76-94-97)	4	3	8	.273
Baylor (77-78)	2	0	4	.000
Boston College (53-60-61-67)	4	6	8	.429
Bradley (50-56)	2	2	4	.333
Brigham Young (68-71)	2	1	4	.200
California (47-57-80-88-92)	5	10	6	.625
Cal St. Fullerton (75-79-82-84-88-90-92-94-95-99-01)	11	25	18	.581
Cal St. Los Angeles (77)	1	2	2	.500
Citadel (90)	1	1	2	.333
Clemson (58-59-76-77-80-91-95-96-00-02)	10	9	20	.310
Colgate (55)	1	1	2	.333
Colorado St. (50)	1	0	2	.000
Connecticut (57-59-65-72-79)	5	3	10	.231
Creighton (91)	1	2	2	.500
Dartmouth (70)	1	1	2	.333
Delaware (70)	1	0	2	.000
Duke (52-53-61)	3	3	6	.333
Eastern Mich. (75-76)	2	4	4	.500
Florida (88-91-96-98)	4	5	8	.385
Florida St. (57-62-63-65-70-75-80-86-87-89-91-92-94-95-96-98-99-00)	18	25	36	.410
Fresno St. (59-88-91)	3	4	6	.400
Georgia (87-90-01)	3	4	5	.444
Georgia Southern (73-90)	2	1	4	.200
Georgia Tech (94-02)	2	4	3	.571
Harvard (68-71-73-74)	4	1	8	.111
Hawaii (80)	1	3	2	.600
Holy Cross (52-58-62-63)	4	9	7	.563
Houston (53-67)	2	3	4	.429
Indiana St. (86)	1	0	2	.000

Team (Years Participated)	Appearances	Won	Lost	Pct
Iowa (72)	1	0	2	.000
Iowa St. (57-70)	2	3	4	.429
Ithaca (62)	1	1	2	.333
James Madison (83)	1	0	2	.000
Kansas (93)	1	0	2	.000
Lafayette (53-54-58-65)	4	3	8	.273
Long Beach St. (89-91-93-98)	4	6	8	.429
La.-Lafayette (00)	1	2	2	.500
LSU (86-87-89-90-91-93-94-96-97-98-00)	11	29	13	.690
Loyola Marymount (86)	I	1	2	.333
Maine (64-76-81-82-83-84-86)	7	7	14	.333
Massachusetts (54-69)	2	2	4	.333
Miami (Fla.) (74-78-79-80-81-82-84-85-86-88-89-92-94-95-96-97-98-99-01)	19	43	30	.589
Michigan (53-62-78-80-81-83-84)	7	12	12	.500
Michigan St. (54)	1	3	2	.600
Minnesota (56-60-64-73-77)	5	17	7	.708
Mississippi (56-64-69-72)	4	3	8	.273
Mississippi St. (71-79-81-85-90-97-98)	7	7	14	.333
Missouri (52-54-58-62-63-64)	6	18	11	.621
Nebraska (01-02)	2	0	4	.000
New Hampshire (56)	1	1	2	.333
New Orleans (84)	1	1	2	.333
New York U. (56-69)	2	3	4	.429
North Carolina (60-66-78-89)	4	2	8	.200
North Carolina St. (68)	1	2	2	.500
Northeastern (66)	1	0	2	.000
Northern Colorado (52-53-55-57-58-59-60-61-62-74)	10	3	20	.130
Notre Dame (57-02)	2	3	4	.429
Ohio (70)	1	2	2	.500
Ohio St. (51-65-66-67)	4	9	7	.563
Oklahoma (51-72-73-74-75-76-92-94-95)	9	14	14	.500
Oklahoma St. (5~55-59-60-61-66-67-68-81-82-83-84-85-86-87-90-93-96-99)	19	38	36	.514
Oral Roberts (78)	1	1	2	.333
Oregon (54)	1	0	2	.000
Oregon St. (52)	1	0	2	.000
Penn St. (52-57-59-63-73)	5	8	10	.444
Pepperdine (79-92)	2	7	2	.778
Princeton (51)	1	0	2	.000

The College World Series Record Book

Team (Years Participated)	Appearances	Won	Lost	Pct
Rice (97-99-02)	3	1	6	.143
Rider (67)	1	1	2	.333
Rollins (54)	1	3	2	.600
Rutgers (50)	1	3	2	.600
St. John's (N.Y) (49-60-66-68-78-80)	6	6	12	.333
St. Louis (65)	1	2	2	.500
San Jose St. (00)	1	0	2	.000
Santa Clara (62)	1	4	2	.667
Seton Hall (64-71-74-75)	4	2	8	.200
South Carolina (75-77-81-82-85-02)	6	13	12	.520
Southern California (48-49-51-55-58-60-61-63-64-66-68-70-71-72-73-74-78-95-98-00-01)	21	74	26	.740
Southern Ill. (68-69-71-74-77)	5	12	10	.545
Springfield (51-55)	2	1	4	.200
Stanford (53-67-82-83-85-87-88-90-95-97-99-00-01-02)	14	33	24	.579
Syracuse (61)	1	2	2	.500
Temple (72-77)	2	2	4	.333
Tennessee (51-95-01)	3	8	6	.571
Texas (49-50-52-53-57-61-62-63-65-66-68-70-72-73-74-75-79-81-82-83-84-85-87-89-92-93-00-02)	29	68	49	.596
Texas A&M (51-64-93-99)	4	2	8	.200
Tex-Pan American (71)	1	2	2	.500
Tufts (50)	1	1	2	.333
Tulane (01)	1	1	2	.333
Tulsa (69-71)	2	6	4	.600
UCLA (69-97)	2	0	4	.000
Utah (51)	1	2	2	.500
Wake Forest (49-55)	2	7	3	.700
Washington St. (50-56-65-76)	4	6	8	.429
Western Mich. (52-55-58-59-61-63)	6	9	12	.429
Wichita St. (82-88-89-91-92-93-96)	7	16	11	.593
Wisconsin (50)	1	2	2	.500
Wyoming (56)	1	1	2	.333
Yale (47-48)	2	1	4	.200

World Series Sites

1947-48	Kalamazoo, Michigan
1949	Wichita, Kansas
1950-2002	Omaha, Nebraska

The College World Series Record Book

DIVISION I RECORDS
SINGLE GAME
INDIVIDUAL BATTING

Most At Bats
  7, by 17 players (last time: Ryan Barthelemy, 1b, Florida St. vs. Stanford, 6-18-99)
Most Runs
  5, by three players (last time, Jeff Christensen, lf, Tennessee vs. Georgia, 6-11-01)
Most Hits
  6, Kris Bennett, 3b, Tennessee vs. Georgia, 6-11-01
Most Doubles
  3, by 6 players (last time: Andy Phillips, ss, Alabama vs. Rice, 6-16-99)
Most Triples
  2, by 11 players (last time: Jack Voigt, LSU vs. Florida St., 5-29-87)
Most Home Runs
  3, by two players (Last: Edmund Muth, Stanford vs. La.-Lafayettte, 6-15-00)
Most Inside-the-Park Home Runs
  1, by many players (last time by Chris Burke, ss, Tennessee vs. Georgia, 6-11-01)
Most Grand Slam Home Runs
  1, by many players (last time: David Coffey, Georgia vs. Tennessee, 6-11-01)
Most Total Bases
  12, by three players (last time: Edmund Muth, cf, Stanford vs. La.-Lafayette, 6-15-00)
Hitting for the Cycle
  Jerry Kindall, Minnesota vs. Mississippi, 6-11-56
Most Runs Batted In
  7, by five players (last time: Kris Bennett, 3b, Tennessee vs. Georgia, 6-11-01)
Most Stolen Bases
  4, by three players (last time: Charlton Jimerson, Miami (Fla.) vs Tennessee, 6-14-01)
Most Steals of Home
  1, by many players (last time: Steven Freehan, La.-Lafayette vs. Clemson, 6-14-00)
Most Sacrifice Bunts
  3, by two players (last time: Paul Chamberlain, Northern Colorado vs. Lafayette, 6-14-58)
Most Sacrifice Flies
  2, by many players (last time: Chris O'Riordan, Stanford vs. Texas, 6-17-02)
Most Hit by Pitches
  2, by many players (last time: Doc Brooks, lf, Georgia vs. Tennessee, 6-11-01)

PITCHING - INDIVIDUAL

Most Innings Pitched
  15, Steve Arlin, Ohio State vs. Washington State, 6-10-65
Most Innings Pitched in Relief
  10, Carl Thomas, Arizona vs. Oklahoma State, 6-12-54

Most Hits Allowed
16, Joe Kazura, New Hampshire vs. Mississippi, 6-9-56
Most Runs Allowed
13, Joe Kazura, New Hampshire vs. Mississippi, 6-9-56
Most Earned Runs Allowed
11, by two pitchers (last time: Patrick Hicklen, Tennessee vs. Georgia, 6-11-01)
Most Strikeouts
20, Steve Arlin, Ohio State vs. Washington State, 6-10-65
Most Strikeouts (nine-inning game)
17, Ed Bane, Arizona State vs. Oklahoma, 6-11-72
Most Strikeouts in one inning
4, by several pitchers (last time: Scott Weiss, Stanford vs. Georgia, 6-8-90)
Most Walks
15, James Waldrip, Oklahoma vs. Springfield, 6-14-51
Most Wild Pitches
3, by 13 pitchers (last time: Kevin Lynn, Clemson vs. Stanford, 6-11-00)
Most Hit Batters
3, by three pitchers (last time: Jon McDonald, Florida St. vs. Southern Cal, 6-14-00)
Most Balks
2, by three pitchers (last time: Beau Richardson, Tulane vs. Nebraska, 6-10-01)

FIELDING - INDIVIDUAL

Most Putouts
20, Doug Mirabelli, c, Wichita State vs. Creighton, 6-3-91
Most Assists
11, Cal Meier, Southern California vs. Florida State, 6-18-70
Most Errors
4, by four players (last time: David Denny, Texas vs. Oklahoma State, 6-8-84)
Most Passed Balls
3, by three players (last time: Bryan Kennedy, Long Beach St. vs. Miami, 6-2-98)

BATTING - TEAM

Most Times at Bat
54, Oklahoma St. vs Texas, 6-6-81
Most Times at Bat (nine-inning game)
50, Holy Cross vs. Penn State, 6-15-52
Most Runs
23, by two teams (last time: Arizona State vs. Oklahoma State, 6-5-84)
Most Runs, One Inning
11, by several teams (last time: Cal St. Fullerton vs. LSU, first inning, 6-5-94)
Most Hits
23, by three teams (last time: Southern California vs. Arizona State, 6-6-98)
Most Doubles
7, Arizona State vs. Oklahoma State, 6-5-84

Most Triples
  4, by two teams (last time: Syracuse vs. Northern Colorado, 6-10-61)
Most Home Runs
  8, LSU vs. Southern California, 5-30-98
Most Total Bases
  42, by two teams (last time: Florida State vs. Stanford, 6-18-99)
Most Runs Batted In
  22, Notre Dame vs. Northern Colorado, 6-9-57
Most Walks
  16, Miami (Fla.) vs. UCLA, 5-31-97
Most Stolen Bases
  7, by five teams (last time: Clemson vs. Long Beach State, 6-3-91)
Most Stolen Bases in One Inning
  4, La.-Lafayette vs. Clemson, 6-14-00, fifth inning
Most Sacrifice Bunts
  5, by three teams (last time: California vs. Michigan, 6-1-80)
Most Sacrifice Flies
  3, by eight teams (last time: Texas vs. South Carolina, 6-22-02)

PITCHING - TEAM

Most Earned Runs Allowed
  22, Northern Colorado vs. Notre Dame, 6-9-57
Most Strike Outs
  20, Ohio State vs. Washington State, 6-10-65
Most Strike Outs (nine-inning game)
  19, Clemson vs. Miami (Fla.), 5-31-96
Most Wild Pitches
  6, Long Beach State vs. Arizona State, 6-3-98
Most Hit Batters
  4, by two teams (last time: Stanford vs. LSU, 6-17-00)
Most Balks
  2, by five teams (last time: Tulane vs. Nebraska, 6-10-01)
Most Pitchers Used
  7, by several teams (last time: Nebraska vs. Clemson, 6-16-02)

FIELDING - TEAM

Most assists
  23, by two teams (last time: Arkansas vs. South Carolina, 5-31-85)
Most assists (nine-inning game)
  22, Miami (Fla.) vs. Cal State Fullerton, 5-31-92
Fewest assists
  3, by many teams (last time: South Carolina vs. Texas, 6-14-75)
Most Errors
  9, by two teams (last time: Texas vs. Oklahoma State, 6-8-84)

Most Double Plays
5, by two teams (last time: Florida State vs. Miami, 6-4-95)
Most Triple Plays
1, by three teams (last time: St. John's vs. Hawaii, 6-1-80)
Most Passed Balls
3, by four teams (last time: Long Beach State vs. Miami (Fla.), 6-2-98)

BATTING - BOTH TEAMS

Most Times at Bat
106, Oklahoma State (54) vs. Texas (52), 6-6-81
Most Times at Bat (nine-inning game)
89, Tennessee (49) vs. Miami (Fla.) (40), 6-9-01
Most Runs
35, by two teams (last time: Southern California (21) vs. Arizona State (14), 6-6-98)
Most Hits
41, Tennessee (21) vs. Miami (Fla.) (20), 6-9-01
Most Doubles
9, by four teams (last time: Stanford (5) vs. Cal State Fullerton (4), 6-3-95)
Most Triples
5, New Hampshire (3) vs. Mississippi (2), 6-9-56
Most Home Runs
10, LSU (8) vs. Southern California (2), 5-30-98
Most Total Bases
71, Southern California (42) vs. Arizona State (29), 6-6-98
Most Runs Batted In
34, Southern California (20) vs. Arizona State (14), 6-6-98
Most Walks
25, Oklahoma State (15) vs. Arizona State (10), 6-5-81
Most Stolen Bases
11, Clemson (7) vs. Long Beach St. (4), 6-3-91
Most Caught Stealing
6, Oklahoma State (3) vs. Indiana State (3), 6-1-86
Most Sacrifice Bunts
7, by three teams (last time: California (5) vs. Michigan (2), 6-12-80)
Most Sacrifice Flies
5, Miami (Fla.) (3) vs. LSU (2), 6-8-96

PITCHING - BOTH TEAMS

Most Earned Runs Allowed
34, Tennessee (21) vs. Miami (Fla.) (13), 6-9-01
Most Strike Outs
31, Santa Clara (16) vs. Michigan (15), 6-16-62
Most Strike Outs (nine-inning game)
25, by four teams (last time: LSU (15) vs. Alabama (10), 6-7-97)

Most Hit Batters
  6, Stanford (4) vs. LSU (2), 6-17-00
Most Wild Pitches
  7, Tennessee (5) vs. Miami (Fla.) (2), 6-9-01
Most Balks
  3, Tulane (2) vs. Nebraska (1), 6-10-01
Most Pitchers Used
  13, Nebraska (7) vs. Clemson (6), 6-14-02

FIELDING - BOTH TEAMS

Most Assists
  40, Santa Clara (22) vs. Michigan (18), 6-16-62
Most Assists (nine-inning game)
  36, by two teams (last time: Oklahoma (18) vs. Temple (19), 6-10-72)
Fewest Assists
  8, Iowa (3) vs. Arizona State (5), 6-10-72
Most Errors
  12, Texas (9) vs. Oklahoma State (3), 6-8-84
Most Double Plays
  8, Minnesota (4) vs. Oklahoma State (4), 6-18-60
Most Passed Balls
  4, Clemson (3) vs. Penn State (1), 6-15-59

MISCELLANEOUS RECORDS

Longest Game by Innings
  15, three games (last game: Southern California vs. Florida State, 6-19-70)
Longest Game by Time
  5:00, Oklahoma State vs. Arizona State, 6-5-81 (13 innings)
Longest Game by Time (nine-inning game)
  4:21, Miami (Fla.) vs. Tennessee, 6-9-01
Shortest Game by Innings
  6, South Carolina vs. Eastern Michigan, 6-8-75
Shortest Game by Time
  1:13, South Carolina vs. Eastern Michigan, 6-8-75, 6 innings
Most Players Left on Base by One Team
  19, by two teams (last time: Oklahoma State vs. Arizona State, 6-5-81)
Most Players Left on Base by One Team (nine-inning game)
  17, Springfield vs. Oklahoma, 6-14-51
Most Players Left on Base by Two Teams
  34, Oklahoma State (18) vs. Arizona (16), 6-12-54
Most Players Left on Base by Two Teams (nine-inning game)
  30, Springfield (17) vs. Oklahoma (13), 6-14-41
Fewest Players Left on Base by One Team
  0, Michigan vs. Stanford, 6-11-53

Fewest Players Left on Base by Two Teams
5, by two teams (last time: Stanford (1) vs. Cal State Fullerton (4), 6-13-01)
Most Players Used by One Team
22, by two teams (last time: LSU vs. Cal State Fullerton, 6-5-94)
Most Players Used by Both Teams
42, LSU (22) vs. Cal State Fullerton (20), 6-5-94
Largest Winning Margin
21, Notre Dame vs. Northern Colorado, 6-9-57 (23-2)
Most Runs by a Losing Team
14, Arizona State vs Southern California, 6-6-98 (14-21)
Largest Margin Overcome for Victory
9 (in the 7th inning), Minnesota vs. Southern California, 6-17-60 (12-11, 10 inn.)
Most Runs Scored in an Extra Inning
8, Georgia Tech vs. Florida State, 6-5-94 (12-4, 10 innings)

SERIES RECORDS
BATTING - INDIVIDUAL

Highest Batting Average (minimum 14 at bats)
.714 (10-14), Jim Morris, Notre Dame, 4 games, 1957
Most At Bats
32, Art Moossman, Holy Cross, 7 games, 1952
Most Runs
11, by two players (last time: Chris Powell, Cal State Fullerton, 1992)
Most Hits
15, Jason Lane, Southern California, 6 games, 1998
Most Consecutive Hits
8, by two players (last time: Barry Bonds, Arizona State, 1984)
Most Doubles
4, by 14 players (last time: Matt Murton, Georgia Tech, 2002)
Most Triples
3, by three players (last time: Arthur Ersepke, Southern Cal, 6 games, 1960)
Most Home Runs
4, by seven players (last time: Edmond Muth, Stanford, 4 games, 2000)
Most Leadoff Home Runs
2, Charlton Jimerson, Miami (Fla.), 4 games, 2001
Most Total Bases
31, Jason Lane, Southern California, 6 games, 1998
Highest Slugging Percentage (minimum 15 at bats)
1.267 (19-15), Kevin Brown, Miami (Fla.), 4 games, 2001
Most Runs Batted In
17, Stan Holmes, Arizona State, 6 games, 1981
Most Base on Balls (Since 1975)
8, by nine players (last time: Andrew Beinbrink, Arizona State, 1998)

The College World Series Record Book

Most Stolen Bases
8, by two players (last time: Tommy Hinzo, Arizona, 5 games, 1986)
Most Sacrifice Bunts
4, by six players (last time: Greg Hanolan, Southern California, 6 games, 1998)
Most Sacrifice Flies
3, Jim Ifland, Oklahoma State, 5 games, 1987
Most Hit by Pitch
3, by several players (last time: Ryan Garko, Stanford, 4 games, 2001)

PITCHING - INDIVIDUAL

Lowest Earned Run Average (minimum 18 innings)
0.50 (1-18), by three pitchers (last: Jim Crawford, Arizona State, 2 games, 1972)
Fewest Earned Runs Allowed (minimum 14 innings)
0, by six pitchers (last time: Patrick Ahearne, Pepperdine, 2 games, 1992)
Most Wins
3, by seven pitchers (last time: Greg Brummett, Wichita State, 1989)
Most Losses
2, by many players (last time: Blair Varnes, Florida State, 2 games, 2000)
Most Saves
4, Huston Street, Texas, 2002
Most Appearances
5, by nine players (last time: Jack Krawczyk, Southern California, 1995)
Most Games Started
3, by many players (last time: Dan Naulty, Cal State Fullerton, 1992)
Most Complete Games
3, by 3 players (last time: Greg Swindell, Texas, 1985)
Most Games Finished
5, by 4 players (last time: Jim Newlin, Wichita State, 1989)
Most Innings Pitched
27 2/3, Bob Garibaldi, Santa Clara, 5 games, 1962
Fewest Hits Allowed (minimum 10 innings)
0, Jim Wixson, Oklahoma State, 11 innings, 4 games, 1960
Fewest Hits Allowed (minimum 20 innings)
5, Steve Arlin, Ohio State, 20 2/3 innings, 5 games, 1966
Most Hits Allowed
25, by two players (last time: Stan Jakubowski, Miami (Fla.), 3 games, 1974)
Most Runs Allowed
20, Rob Souza, Miami (Fla.), 2 games, 1984
Most Earned Runs Allowed
15, Ben McDonald, LSU, 3 games, 1989
Fewest Walks Allowed (minimum 15 innings)
0, by two pitchers (last time: Gilbert Heredia, Arizona, 16 innings, 2 games, 1986)
Most Walks Allowed

20, Rod Keogh, Washington State, 2 games, 1950
Most Strikeouts
38, Bob Garibaldi, Santa Clara, 5 games, 1962
Most Wild Pitches
6, Bob Garibaldi, Santa Clara, 5 games, 1962
Most Hit Batters
5, by three pitchers (last time: Jason Young, Stanford, 2 games, 1999)
Most Balks
2, by six pitchers (last time: Beau Richardson, Tulane, 1 game, 2001)

FIELDING - INDIVIDUAL

Most Putouts
79, Tim Wallach, 1b, Cal State Fullerton, 6 games, 1979
Most Assists
32, by two players (last time: P.J. Forbes, 2b, Wichita State, 6 games, 1989)
Most Chances Without an Error
74, Steve Willis, 1b, Arizona State, 6 games, 1988
Most Errors
8, Gary LeFevers, ss, Arizona, 4 games, 1960

BATTING - TEAM

Highest Batting Average (Minimum 4 games)
.394 (63-160), Tennessee, 4 games, 2001
Most At Bats
250, Holy Cross, 7 games, 1952
Most Runs
62, Southern California, 6 games, 1998
Most Runs Per Game (Minimum 4 games)
12.3, Miami, 49 runs in 4 games, 2001
Most Hits
88, Southern California, 6 games, 1998
Most Doubles
18, Oklahoma State, 5 games, 1981
Most Triples
7, by two teams (last time: Missouri, 6 games, 1954)
Most Home Runs
17, by two teams (LSU, Southern California, 1998)
Most Grand Slam Home Runs
2, by three teams (last time: Stanford, 4 games, 2000)
Most Total Bases
152, Southern California, 6 games, 1998
Highest Slugging Percentage (Minimum 4 games)
.683 (99-145), LSU, 4 games, 1998
Most Runs Batted In

61, Southern California, 6 games, 1998
Most Walks
55, Southern California, 6 games, 1960
Fewest Strikeouts (Minimum 4 games)
12, Texas, 4 games, 1992
Most Strikeouts
57, Southern California, 5 games, 1970
Most Stolen Bases
17, Oklahoma State, 5 games
Most Sacrifice Bunts
12, Santa Clara, 6 games, 1962
Most Sacrifice Flies
5, by two teams (last time: Cal State Fullerton, 6 games, 1979)
Most Hit Batters
8, Missouri, 5 games, 1952

PITCHING - TEAM

Lowest Earned Run Average (Minimum 4 games)
0.60, California, 5 games, 1957 (3-45)
Most Innings Pitched
63, Santa Clara, 6 games, 1962
Most Shutouts
3, by four teams (last time: Arizona State, 6 games, 1972)
Most Consecutive Scoreless Innings
31, Arizona State, 1972
Most Consecutive Scoreless Innings at Start of CWS
24 1/3, Pepperdine, 1992
Most Complete Games
7, Holy Cross, 7 games, 1952
Most Saves
4, Texas, 4 games, 2002
Fewest Hits Allowed (Minimum 4 games)
16, Oklahoma State, 4 games, 1960
Most Hits Allowed
73, Southern California, 6 games, 1995
Fewest Runs Allowed (Minimum 4 games)
3, California, 5 games, 1957
Most Runs Allowed
58, Oklahoma State, 5 games, 1984
Most Earned Runs Allowed
47, Oklahoma State, 5 games, 1984
Fewest Walks Allowed (Minimum 4 games)
3, Cal State Fullerton, 4 games, 2001

Most Walks Allowed
41, Oklahoma State, 5 games, 1984
Most Strikeouts
77, Arizona State, 6 games, 1967
Most Wild Pitches
10, Santa Clara, 6 games, 1962
Most Hit Batters
9, Stanford, 4 games, 1997
Most Balks
3, LSU, 4 games, 2000

FIELDING - TEAM
Highest Fielding Percentage (Minimum 4 games)
.993, LSU, 4 games, 1991 (108-39-1)
Most Assists
88, by two teams (last time: Wichita State, 6 games, 1989)
Most Errors
18, Tulsa, 5 games, 1971
Most Double Plays
12, Stanford, 6 games, 1987
Most Triple Plays
1, by three teams (last time: St. John's, 3 games, 1980)

CAREER RECORDS
BATTING
Highest Batting Average (minimum 29 at bats)
.517, by two players (last time: Jason Lane, Southern California, 1998)
Most Games Played
20, Daryl Arenstein, Southern California, 1970-71-72-73
Most At Bats
68, Daryl Arenstein, Southern California, 1970-71-72-73
Most Runs
21, Bill Bates, Texas, 1983-84-85
Most Hits
23, Keith Moreland, Texas, 1973-74-75
Most Doubles
7, Robin Ventura, Oklahoma State, 1986-87
Most Triples
3, by five players (last time: Spike Owen, Texas, 1981-82)
Most Home Runs
6, Edmund Muth, Stanford, 1997-99-00
Most Grand Slam Home Runs
2, Mark Kotsay, Cal State Fullerton, 1994-95
Most Total Bases

37, Marshall McDougall, Florida State, 1999-00
Highest Slugging Percentage (minimum 29 at bats)
1.103 (32-29), Mark Kotsay, Cal State Fullerton, 1994-95
Most Runs Batted In
20, Bob Horner, Arizona State, 1976-77-78
Most Stolen Bases
11, Doug Dascenzo, Oklahoma State, 1984-85
Most Sacrifice Bunts
7, Paul Merch, Oklahoma State, 1959-60-61
Most Sacrifice Flies
3, by two players (last time: Jim Ifland, Oklahoma State, 1986-87)
Most Hit by Pitches
6, Ryan Garko, Stanford, 2001-02

PITCHING - INDIVIDUAL

Lowest Earned Run Average (minimum 20 innings)
0.00, by two pitchers (last time: Jim Crawford, Arizona State, 1969-72)
Lowest Earned Run Average (minimum 30 innings)
0.96 (5-47), Steve Arlin, Ohio State, 1965-66
Most Wins
4, by nine pitchers (last time: Greg Brummett, Wichita State, 1988-89)
Most No-Hitters
1, by two pitchers (last time: Jim Wixson, Oklahoma St. vs. No. Carolina, 6-15-60)
Most One-Hitters (nine-inning game)
1, by 11 pitchers (last time: Alan Dunn & Tim Meacham, Alabama vs. Arizona State, 6-10-83)
Most One-Hitters (extra-inning game)
1, Rod Keogh, Washington State vs. Rutgers, 6-19-50
Most Years With Wins
3, by three players (last time: Allan Westfall, Miami (Fla.), 1994-95-96)
Most Losses
4, Ben McDonald, LSU, 1987-89
Most Saves
4, by four pitchers (last time: Huston Street, Texas, 2002)
Most Appearances
10, Rick Raether, Miami (Fla.), 1985-86
Most Games Started
7, J.D. Arteaga, Miami (Fla.), 1994-95-96-97
Most Complete Games
4, by four pitchers (last time: Greg Swindell, Texas, 1984-85)
Most Games Finished
9, Rick Raether, Miami (Fla.), 1985-86
Most Innings Pitched

47, by two players (last time: Greg Swindell, Texas, 1984-85)
Fewest Hits Allowed (minimum 20 innings)
7, by two pitchers (last time: Kevin Dukes, Arizona State, 22 innings, 1981)
Fewest Hits Allowed (minimum 30 innings)
16, by two pitchers (last time: Steve Arlin, Ohio State, 47 innings, 1965-66)
Most Hits Allowed
51, J.D. Arteaga, Miami (Fla.), 1994-94-96-97
Most Runs Allowed
29, Bill Swift, Maine, 1981-82-83-84
Most Earned Runs Allowed
22, Bill Swift, Maine, 1981-82-83-84
Most Strikeouts
64, Carl Thomas, Arizona, 1954-55-56
Fewest Walks (minimum 20 innings)
3, by five pitchers (last time: Bob Chalk, Arizona, 20 1/3 innings, 1976)
Fewest Walks (minimum 30 innings)
5, by two pitchers (last time: Mark Barr, Southern California, 32 1/3 innings, 1973-74)
Most Walks
27, Dennis Livingston, Oklahoma State, 1982-83-84
Most Wild Pitches
6, Bob Garibaldi, Santa Clara, 1962
Most Hit Batters
7, Jason Young, Stanford, 1999-00
Most Balks
3, Frank Carbajal, Northern Colorado, 1959-60

FIELDING - INDIVIDUAL
Most Putouts
191, Daryl Arenstein, 1b, Southern California, 1970-71-72-73
Most Assists
57, Bill Bates, 2b, Texas, 1983-84-85
Most Chances Without Committing an Error
86, Kelly Snider, 1b, Oklahoma, 1974-75-76
Most Chances Without Committing an Error
10, by two players (last time: Roy Smalley, ss, Southern California, 1972-73)

Championship Game Records
BATTING - INDIVIDUAL
Most At Bats
7, by five players (last time: Wes Rachels, Southern Cal vs. Arizona St., 6-6-98)
Most At Bats (nine-inning game)
7, Wes Rachels, Southern California vs. Arizona State, 6-6-98

The College World Series Record Book

Most Runs
4, by two players (last time: Warren Morris, LSU vs. Miami (Fla.), 6-8-96)
Most Hits
5, by three players (last time: Wes Rachels and Jeremy Freitas, Southern California vs. Arizona State, 6-6-98)
Most Doubles
2. by six players (last time: Omar Quintanilla, Texas vs. South Carolina, 6-22-02)
Most Triples
2, by two players (last time: G.J. Cantu, Houston vs. Arizona State, 6-18-67)
Most Home Runs
2, by three players (last time: Robb Gorr, So. Cal vs. Arizona State, 6-6-98)
Most Total Bases
10, Bill Horning, Minnesota vs. Arizona, 6-14-56
Most Runs Batted In
7, Wes Rachels, Southern California vs. Arizona State, 6-6-98
Most Stolen Bases
3, Billy Hall, Wichita State vs. LSU, 6-8-91
Most Sacrifice Bunts
2, by four players (last time: Michael Collins, Arizona St. vs. Southern California, 6-6-98)
Most Sacrifice Flies
2, by two players (last time: Ryan Hubele, Texas vs. South Carolina, 6-22-02)
Most Hit by Pitch
2, Anthony Blackmon, Oklahoma State vs. Stanford, 6-7-87

PITCHING - INDIVIDUAL

Most Innings Pitched
10, Jim Rantz, Minnesota vs. Southern California, 6-20-60
Most Innings Pitched in Relief
8 2/3, Kevin Dukes, Arizona State vs. Oklahoma State, 6-8-81
Fewest Hits Allowed
3, by three players (last time: Brett Laxton, LSU vs. Wichita State, 6-12-93)
Most Hits Allowed
12, by two players (last time: Jack McDowell, Stanford vs. Oklahoma State, 6-7-87)
Complete-Game Shutouts
1, by three players (last time: Brett Laxton, LSU vs. Wichita State, 6-12-93)
Most Home Runs Allowed
10, Steve Rogers, Tulsa vs. Arizona State, 6-20-69
Most Earned Runs Allowed
8, Steve Rogers, Tulsa vs. Arizona State, 6-20-69
Most Strikeouts
16, Brett Laxton, LSU vs. Wichita State, 6-12-93
Most Base on Balls Allowed

12, Rod Keogh, Washington State vs. Texas
Most Wild Pitches
3, by three pitchers (last time: Patrick Coogan, LSU vs. Alabama, 6-7-97)
Most Hit Batters
2, by several pitchers (last time: Justin Simmons, Texas vs. So. Carolina, 6-22-02)
Most Balks
1, by three pitchers (last time: Aaron Rawl, South Carolina vs. Texas, 6-22-02)
Most Championship Game Wins, Career
2, Jim Ehrler, Texas, 1949-50
Most Championship Game Starts, Career
2, Jim Ehrler, Texas, 1949-50
Most Championship Game Losses, Career
2, Robert Goodyear, 1947-48

FIELDING - INDIVIDUAL

Most Putouts
18, Doug Kasimer, 1b, Florida State vs. Southern California, 6-19-70
Most Putouts (nine-inning game)
16, by three players (last time: Adrian Antonini, c, LSU vs. Wichita State, 6-12-93)
Most Assists
11, Cal Meier, ss, Southern California vs. Florida State, 6-19-70
Most Assists (nine-inning game)
8, Roger Wich, ss, Oklahoma vs. Tennessee, 6-17-51
Most Errors
3, by three players (last time: Art Toombs, ss, Houston vs. Arizona State, 6-18-67)
Most Passed Balls
2, by six players (last time: Greg Halvorson, Arizona St. vs. Southern Cal, 6-6-98)

BATTING - TEAM

Most At Bats
52, Southern California vs. Florida State, 6-19-70
Most At Bats (nine-inning game)
46, Southern California vs. Arizona State, 6-6-98
Most Runs
21, Southern California vs. Arizona State, 6-6-98
Most Runs, One Inning
7, Southern California vs. Missouri, 4th inning, 6-19-58
Most Hits
23, Southern California vs. Arizona State, 6-6-98
Most Doubles
5, Texas vs. South Carolina, 6-22-02
Most Triples
3, by two teams (last time: Ohio State vs. Oklahoma State, 6-18-66)

Most Home Runs
5, Southern California vs. Arizona State, 6-6-98
Most Total Bases
42, Southern California vs. Arizona State, 6-6-98
Most Runs Batted In
20, Southern California vs. Arizona State, 6-6-98
Most Walks
14, Texas vs. Washington State, 6-23-50
Fewest Strikeouts
1, Southern California vs. Arizona State, 6-8-78
Most Stolen Bases
4, by two teams (last time: Wichita State vs. LSU, 6-8-91)
Most Sacrifice Bunts
4, Cal State Fullerton vs. Southern California, 6-10-95
Most Sacrifice Flies
3, Miami vs. LSU, 6-8-96

PITCHING - TEAM

Fewest Hits Allowed
3, by five teams (last time: LSU vs. Wichita State, 6-12-93)
Fewest Runs Allowed
0, by five teams (last time: LSU vs. Wichita State, 6-12-93)
Most Earned Runs Allowed
21, Arizona State vs. Southern California, 6-6-98
Most Unearned Runs Allowed
8, Southern California vs. Cal State Fullerton, 6-10-95
Fewest Base on Balls Allowed
0, by six teams (last time: Cal State Fullerton vs. Southern Cal, 6-10-95)
Most Strikeouts
16, by two teams (last time: LSU vs. Wichita State, 6-12-93)
Most Strikeouts (nine-inning game)
16, LSU vs. Wichita State, 6-12-93
Most Hit Batters
4, Stanford vs. LSU, 6-17-00
Most Wild Pitches
3, by three teams (Alabama vs. LSU, 6-7-97)
Most Balks
1, by three teams (last time: South Carolina vs. Texas, 6-22-02)
Most Pitchers Used
7, Nebraska vs. Clemson, 6-14-02

FIELDING - TEAM

Most Assists
23, Southern California vs. Florida State, 6-19-70

The College World Series Record Book

Most Assists (nine-inning game)
20, Arizona vs. Hawaii, 6-15-80
Most Errors
6, by two teams (last time: Houston vs. Arizona State, 6-18-67)
Most Double Plays
4, Stanford vs. Oklahoma State, 6-7-87
Most Passed Balls
2, by seven teams (last time: Arizona State vs. Southern Cal, 6-6-98)

BATTING - BOTH TEAMS

Most At Bats
102, Southern California (52) vs. Florida State. (50), 6-19-70 (15 innings)
Most At Bats (nine-inning game)
87, Southern California (46) vs. Arizona State (41), 6-6-98
Most Runs
35, Southern California (21) vs. Arizona State (14), 6-6-98
Most Hits
39, Southern California (23) vs. Arizona State (16), 6-6-98
Most Doubles
8, Texas (5) vs. South Carolina (3), 6-22-02
Most Triples
3, by two teams (last time: Ohio State (3) vs. Oklahoma State (0), 6-18-66)
Most Home Runs
9, Southern California (5) vs. Arizona State (4), 6-6-98
Most Total Bases
71, Southern California (42) vs. Arizona State (29), 6-6-98
Most Runs Batted In
34, Southern California (20) vs. Arizona State (14), 6-6-98
Most Walks
18, by two teams (last time: Southern California (9) vs. Minnesota (9), 6-20-60)
Fewest Strikeouts
3, Southern California (1) vs. Arizona State (2), 6-8-78
Most Stolen Bases
5, by three teams (last time: Arizona vs. Florida State, 6-9-86)
Most Sacrifice Bunts
5, by two teams (last time: Cal State Fullerton (4) vs. Southern California (1), 6-10-95)
Most Sacrifice Flies
5, Miami (Fla.) (3) vs. LSU (2), 6-8-96

PITCHING - BOTH TEAMS

Fewest Hits Allowed
8, by three teams (last time: Cal State Fullerton (3) vs. Texas (5), 6-10-84)
Fewest Runs Allowed
1, by three teams (last time: Southern California (0) vs. Arizona State (1), 6-16-72)

Fewest Earned Runs Allowed
  0, Southern California (0), Arizona State (0), 6-16-72
Most Earned Runs Allowed
  32, Arizona State (21) vs. Southern California (11), 6-6-98
Most Unearned Runs Allowed
  11, Southern California (8) vs. Cal State Fullerton (3), 6-10-95
Fewest Bases on Balls Allowed
  1, by two teams (last time: Arizona State (0) vs. South Carolina (1), 6-18-77)
Most Strikeouts
  31, Santa Clara (16) vs. Michigan (15), 6-16-62
Most Strikeouts (nine-inning game)
  25, LSU (15) vs. Alabama (10), 6-7-97
Most Wild Pitches
  4, Alabama (3) vs. LSU (1), 6-7-97
Most Hit Batters
  6, Stanford (4) vs. LSU (2), 6-17-00
Most Balks
  1, by three teams (last time: LSU (1) vs. Stanford (0), 6-17-00)
Most Pitchers Used
  10, Southern California (5) vs. Arizona State (5), 6-6-98

FIELDING - TEAMS

Most Assists
  40, Santa Clara (22) vs. Michigan (18), 6-16-62
Most Assists (nine-inning game)
  36, Oklahoma (18) vs. Georgia Tech (18), 6-11-94
Most Errors
  8, by three teams (last time: Houston (6) vs. Arizona State (2), 6-18-67)
Most Double Plays
  6, Stanford (4) vs. Oklahoma State (2), 6-7-87
Most Passed Balls
  3, Texas (2) vs. Miami (Fla.) (1), 6-11-85

MISCELLANEOUS RECORDS

Longest Game by Innings
  15, two games (last time: Southern California vs. Florida State, 6-19-70)
Longest Game by Time
  3:59, Southern California vs. Arizona State, 6-6-98
Longest game by Time (nine-inning game)
  3:59, Southern California vs. Arizona State, 6-6-98
Shortest Game by Time
  1:35, Arizona State vs. South Carolina, 6-18-77

Most Runners Left on Base by One Team
16, by two teams (last time: Oklahoma vs. Tennessee, 6-17-51)
Fewest Runners Left on Base by One Team
2, by two teams (last time: Cal State Fullerton vs. Arkansas, 6-8-79)
Most Runners Left on Base by Both Teams
25, Michigan (13) vs. Texas (12), 6-16-53
Fewest Runners Left on Base by Both Teams
8, by two teams (last time: Cal State (2) vs. Arkansas (6), 6-8-79)
Most Players Used by One Team
19, Stanford vs. Miami (Fla.), 6-16-01
Most Players Used by Both Teams
34, Georgia Tech (18) vs. Oklahoma (16), 6-11-94
Largest Winning Margin
11, by two teams (last time: Miami (Fla.) vs. Stanford, 6-16-01)
Largest Margin Overcome for Victory
4, by two teams (last time: LSU vs. Miami (Fla.), 6-8-96)
Most Appearances by One School in Championship Game
14, Southern California

COACHING RECORDS

Appearances
17, Cliff Gustafson, Texas
Games
76, Rod Dedeaux, Southern California
Titles
10, Rod Dedeaux, Southern California
Most Consecutive Titles
5, Rod Dedeaux, Southern California, 1970, 71, 72, 73, 74
Winning Percentage
.789 (60-16) Rod Dedeaux, Southern California
Victories
60, Rod Dedeaux, Southern California
Coaching Most Different Teams in the CWS
3, Larry Cochell (Oral Roberts, 1978; Cal State Fullerton, 1988, 1990; and Oklahoma, 1992, 1994, 1995); Ron Polk (Georgia Southern, 1973; Mississippi State, 1979, 1981, 1985, 1990, 1997; Georgia, 2001)
Taken Team to Omaha First Six Years At That School
Jim Morris (Miami of Florida, 1994-99)

The College World Series Record Book
Attendance Records
Attendance, Total, Series - 223,762 in 2002
Attendance, Average Per Session, Series - 22,376 (2002)
Attendance, Single Session - 25,581, June 16, 2002

Year	Sessions	Total Attend.	Avg. per session	Year	Sessions	Total Attend.	Avg. per session
1947	2	3,792	1,896	1973	9	65,356	6,262
1948	2	3,352	1,676	1974	10	71,105	7,111
1949	4	n/a*	n/a*	1975	10	78,052	7,805
1950	10	17,805	1,781	1976	10	83,455	8,346
1951	9	27,789	3,088	1977	10	90,117	9,012
1952	10	38,731	3,873	1978	9	79,654	8,850
1953	10	31,990	3,199	1979	10	87,070	8,707
1954	10	35,403	3,540	1980	10	95,406	9,541
1955	10	21,843	2,184	1981	10	120,535	12,054
1956	10	29,940	2,994	1982	9	106,144	11,794
1957	9	26,609	2,957	1983	9	115,700	12,856
1958	10	25,931	2,593	1984	10	120,456	12,046
1959	10	33,607	3,361	1985	10	125,970	12,597
1960	10	35,222	3,522	1986	10	124,958	12,496
1961	9	24,778	2,753	1987	10	130,659	13,066
1962	10	39,307	3,391	1988	9	132,698	14,744
1963	10	52,757	5,276	1989	9	132,865	14,763
1964	10	61,871	6,187	1990	9	138,426	15,381
1965	10	45,894	4,589	1991	9	133,763	14,863
1966	10	63,376	6,338	1992	10	154,216	15.422
1967	10	63,906	6,391	1993	10	173,296	17,330
1968	9	58,373	6,486	1994	9	161,638	17,960
1969	10	63,265	6,327	1995	10	182,759	18,276
1970	10	74,683	7,468	1996	9	182,430	20,270
1971	10	77,460	7,746	1997	10	204,309	20,431
1972	10	80,214	8,021	1998	10	204,361	20,436
				1999	10	206,639	20,664
				2000	9	200,917	22,324
				2001	9	196,515	21,835
				2002	10	223,762	22,376

*No attendance figures were available for the 1949 championship held in Wichita, Kansas.

The all-time attendance figure exceeded five million fans in 2002.

All-Time Teams
All-Time Team (1947-1970)
First Team
1b - John Boccabella, Santa Clara, 1962
2b - Dewey Markus, Minnesota, 1964
3b - Sal Bando, Arizona St., 1965
ss - Woody Woodward, Florida St., 1963
of - Ron Fairley, So. Cal, 1958
of - Tom Paciorek, Houston, 1968
of - John Dolinsek, Arizona St., 1969
c - Bud Hollowell, So. Cal, 1963
p - Steve Arlin, Ohio St., 1965, 66
p - Burt Hooton, Texas, 1969, 70

Second Team
1b - Bill Seinsoth, So. Cal, 1968
2b - Frank Quilici, W. Michigan, 1961
3b - Bob Lillis, So. Cal, 1951
ss - Don Kessinger, Mississippi, 1964
of - John Turco, Holy Cross, 1952
of - Jim Morris, Notre Dame, 1957
of - Bob Fry, Washington St., 1965
c - Tom Yewcic, Michigan St., 1965
p - Jim O'Neill, Holy Cross, 1952
p - Bob Garibaldi, Santa Clara, 1962

Note: Team selected by blue-ribbon committee chaired by Abe Chanin as part of the 25th CWS celebration in 1971.

All-Time Team (1947-1995)
First Team
c - Mike Day, Oklahoma St., 1982, 83, 84, 85
1b - Will Clark, Mississippi St., 1985
2b - Todd Walker, LSU, 1993, 94
3b - Robin Ventura, Oklahoma St., 1986, 87
ss - Spike Owen, Texas, 1981, 82
of - Barry Bonds, Arizona St., 1983, 84
of - Mark Kotsay, Cal St. Fullerton, 1994, 95
of - Dave Winfield, Minnesota, 1973
dh - Pete Incaviglia, Oklahoma St., 1983, 84, 85
p - Steve Arlin, Ohio St., 1965, 66
p - Burt Hooton, Texas, 1969, 70
Head Coach - Rod Dedeaux, So. Cal, 1951, 55, 58, 60, 61, 63, 64, 66, 68, 70, 71, 72, 73, 74, 78

Note: Team selected by readers of the Omaha World-Herald as part of the 50th CWS celebration in 1996.

All-Decade Teams
1940s-50s
p - Tom Borland, Oklahoma St., 1954, 55
p - James O'Neill, Holy Cross, 1952
c - Alan Hall, Arizona, 1958, 59, 60
1b - Sonny Siebert, Missouri, 1958
2b - Stanley Charnofsky, So. Cal, 1951
ss - Charles Shoemaker, Arizona, 1959, 60
3b - Ken Komodzinski, Holy Cross, 1958
of - Jim Morris, Notre Dame, 1957
of - John Turco, Holy Cross, 1952
of - Ray VanCleef, Rutgers, 1950

1960s
p - Steve Arlin, Ohio St., 1965, 66
p - Burt Hooton, Texas, 1969, 70
c - Chuck Brinkman, Ohio St., 1965, 66
1b - Bill Seinsoth, So. Cal, 1968
2b - Lou Bagwell, Texas, 1968, 69, 70
ss - Danny Thompson, Oklahoma St., 1968
3b - Sal Bando, Arizona St., 1964, 65
of - John Dolinsek, Arizona St., 1969
of - Scott Reid, Arizona St., 1967
of - Wayne Weatherly, Oklahoma St., 1966, 68

1970s
p - Eddie Bane, Arizona St,, 1972, 73
p - Russ McQueen, So. Cal, 1972, 73
c - Chris Bando, Arizona St., 1977, 78
1b - Jerry Tabb, Tulsa, 1971
2b - Bob Horner, Arizona St., 1976, 77, 78
ss - Roy Smalley, So. Cal, 1972, 73
3b - Keith Moreland, Texas, 1973, 74, 75
of - Fred Lynn, So.Cal, 1971, 72, 73
of - Kevin McReynolds, Arkansas, 1979
of - Dave Winfield, Minnesota, 1973
dh - Steve Powers, Arizona, 1976

1980s
p - Greg Brummett, Wichita State, 1988, 89
p - Craig Lefferts, Arizona, 1979, 80
c - Mike Day, Oklahoma State, 1982, 84, 85
1b - Will Clark, Mississippi State, 1985
2b - Bill Bates, Texas, 1983, 84, 85
ss - Spike Owen, Texas, 1981, 82
3b - Robin Ventura, Oklahoma St., 1986, 87
of - Barry Bonds, Arizona St., 1983, 84
of - Terry Francona, Arizona, 1979, 80
of - Stan Holmes, Arizona St., 1981
dh - Pete Incaviglia, Oklahoma St., 1983, 84, 85

1990-95
p - Patrick Ahearne, Pepperdine, 1992
p - Mike Rebhan, Georgia, 1990
c - Gary Hymel, LSU, 1990, 91
1b - Doug Mientkiewicz, Florida St., 1995
2b - Todd Walker, LSU, 1993, 94
ss - Nomar Garciaparra, Georgia Tech, 1994
3b - Phil Nevin, Cal St. Fullerton, 1992
of - J.D. Drew, Florida State, 1995
of - Geoff Jenkins, Southern Cal, 1995
of - Mark Kotsay, Cal State Fullerton, 1994, 95
dh - Lyle Mouton, LSU, 1990, 91

Head Coaches
Jim Brock, Arizona St., 1972, 73, 75, 76, 77, 78, 81, 83, 84, 87, 88, 93, 94
Rod Dedeaux, Southern Cal, 1951, 55, 58, 60 61, 63, 64, 66, 68, 70, 71, 72, 73, 74, 78
Augie Garrido, Cal St. Fullerton, 1975, 79, 82, 84, 92, 94, 95
Cliff Gustafson, Texas, 1968, 69, 70, 72, 73, 74, 75, 79, 81, 82, 83, 84, 85, 87, 89, 92, 93
Gene Stephenson, Wichita State, 1982, 88, 89, 91, 92, 93

Note: Teams selected as part of 50th CWS celebration in 1996 by a panel of 60 voters representing CWS head coaches, media who covered the event and chairs of the Division I Baseball Committee.

1996-2002
p - J.D. Arteaga, Miami (Fla.), 1996, 97
p - Jack Krawczyk, Southern Cal, 1998
c - Eric Munson, Southern Cal, 1998
1b - Kevin Brown, Miami (Fla.), 1999, 2001
2b - Marshall McDougall, Florida St., 1999
ss - Brandon Larson, LSU, 1997
3b - Pat Burrell, Miami (Fla.), 1996, 97, 98
of - Charlton Jimerson, Miami (Fla.), 2001
of - Edmund Muth, Stanford, 2000
of - Manny Crespo, Miami (Fla.), 1999

NOTE: Team selected by Madden Publishing Company.

The College World Series Record Book

All-Time Coaching Records by School

	Appearances	Won	Lost	Pct.
Alabama				
Tilden Campbell (1950)	1	1	2	.333
Barry Shollenberger (1983)	1	3	2	.600
Jim Wells (1996, 97, 99)	3	7	6	.538
Arizona				
Frank Sancet (1954, 55, 56, 58, 59, 60, 63, 66, 70)	9	17	18	.486
Jerry Kindall (1976, 79, 80, 85, 86)	5	15	7	.682
Arizona State				
Bobby Winkles (1964, 65, 67, 69)	4	16	5	.762
Jim Brock (1972, 73, 75, 76, 77, 78, 81 83, 84, 87, 88, 93, 94)	13	36	24	.600
Pat Murphy (1998)	1	3	1	.750
Arkansas				
Norm DeBriyn (1979, 85, 87, 89)	4	7	8	.467
Auburn				
Paul Nix (1967, 76)	2	2	4	.333
Hal Baird (1994, 97)	2	1	4	.200
Baylor				
Mickey Sullivan (1977, 78)	2	0	4	.000
Boston College				
John Tempoe (1953)	1	2	2	.500
Ed Peligrini (1960, 61, 67)	3	4	6	.400
Bradley				
Leo Schrall (1950, 56)	2	2	4	.333
Brigham Young				
Glen Tuckett (1968, 71)	2	1	4	.200
California				
Clint Evans (1947)	1	2	0	1.000
George Wolfman (1957)	1	5	0	1.000
Bob Milano (1980, 88, 92)	3	3	6	.333
Cal State Fullerton				
Augie Garrido (1975, 79, 82, 84, 92, 94, 95)	7	20	10	.667
Larry Cochell (1988, 90)	2	2	4	.333
George Horton (1999, 01)	2	3	4	.429
Cal State Los Angeles				
Jack Deutsch (1977)	1	2	2	.500

The College World Series Record Book

	Appearances	Won	Lost	Pct.
Citadel				
Chal Port (1990)	1	1	2	.333
Clemson				
Bill Wilhelm (1958, 59, 76, 77, 80, 91)	6	4	12	.250
Jack Leggett (1995, 96, 00, 02)	4	5	7	.417
Colgate				
Red O'Hora (1955)	1	1	2	.333
Colorado State				
Mark Duncan (1950)	1	0	2	.000
Connecticut				
J.O. Christian (1957, 59)	2	1	4	.200
Larry Panciera (1965, 72, 79)	3	2	6	.250
Creighton				
Jim Hendry (1991)	1	2	2	.500
Dartmouth				
Tony Lupien (1970)	1	1	2	.500
Delaware				
Bob Hannah (1970)	1	1	2	.333
Duke				
Jack Coombs (1952)	1	1	2	.333
Ace Parker (1953, 61)	2	2	4	.333
Eastern Michigan				
Ron Oestrike (1975, 76)	2	4	4	.500
Florida				
Joe Arnold (1988, 91)	2	3	4	.429
Andy Lopez (1996, 98)	2	2	4	.333
Florida State				
Dan Litwhiler (1957, 62, 63)	3	3	5	.333
Fred Hatfield (1965)	1	1	2	.333
Jack Stallings (1970)	1	4	2	.667
Woody Woodward (1975)	1	0	2	.000
Mike Martin (1980, 86, 87, 89, 91, 92, 94, 95, 96, 98, 99, 00)	12	17	24	.415
Fresno State				
Pete Beiden (1959)	1	3	2	.600
Bob Bennett (1988, 91)	2	1	4	.200
Georgia				
Steve Webber (1987, 90)	2	4	3	.571
Ron Polk (2001)	1	0	2	.000
Georgia Southern				
Ron Polk (1973)	1	1	2	.333

The College World Series Record Book

	Appearances	Won	Lost	Pct.
Jack Stallings (1990)	1	0	2	.000
Georgia Tech				
Danny Hall (1994, 02)	1	4	3	..571
Harvard				
Loyal Park (1968, 71, 73, 74)	4	1	8	.111
Hawaii				
Les Murakami (1980)	1	3	2	.600
Holy Cross				
Jack Barry (1952, 58)	2	8	3	.727
Albert Riopel (1962, 63)	2	1	4	.200
Houston				
Lovette Hill (1953, 67)	2	3	4	.429
Indiana State				
Bob Warn (1986)	1	0	2	.000
Iowa				
Duane Banks (1972)	1	0	2	.000
Iowa State				
Cap Timm (1957, 70)	2	3	4	.429
Ithaca				
Bucky Freeman (1962)	1	1	2	.333
James Madison				
Brad Babcock (1983)	1	0	2	.000
Kansas				
Dave Bingham (1993)	1	0	2	.000
Lafayette				
Charlie Gelbert (1953, 54, 58, 65)	4	3	8	.273
Long Beach State				
Dave Snow (1989, 91, 93, 98)	4	6	8	.429
Louisiana-Lafayette				
Tony Robichaux (2000)	1	2	2	.500
Louisiana State University				
Skip Bertman (1986, 87, 89, 90, 91, 93, 94, 96, 97, 98, 00)	11	29	13	.690
Loyola Marymount				
Dave Snow (1986)	1	1	2	.333
Maine				
John Butterfield (1964)	1	3	2	.600
John Winkin (1976, 81, 82, 83, 84, 86)	6	4	12	.250
Massachusetts				
Dick Bergquist (1954, 69)	2	2	4	.333

The College World Series Record Book

	Appearances	Won	Lost	Pct.
Miami (Florida)				
Ron Fraser (1974, 78, 79, 80, 81, 82 84, 85, 86, 88, 89, 92)	12	26	21	.553
Jim Morris (1994, 95, 96, 97, 98, 99, 01)	7	17	9	.654
Michigan				
Ray Fisher (1953)	1	4	1	.800
Don Lund (1962)	1	4	1	.800
Moby Benedict (1978)	1	1	2	.333
Bud Middaugh (1980, 81, 83, 84)	4	3	8	.273
Michigan State				
Danny Litwhiler (1954)	1	3	2	.600
Minnesota				
Dick Siebert (1956, 60, 64, 73, 77)	5	17	7	.708
Mississippi				
Tom Swayze (1956, 64, 69)	3	3	6	.333
Mississippi State				
Paul Gregory (1971)	1	0	2	.000
Ron Polk (1979, 81, 85, 90, 97)	5	6	10	.375
Pat McMahon (1998)	1	1	2	.333
Missouri				
Hi Simmons (1952, 54, 58, 62, 63, 64)	6	18	11	.621
Nebraska				
Dave Van Horn (2001, 02)	2	0	4	.000
New Hampshire				
Hank Swasey (1956)	1	1	2	.333
New Orleans				
Ron Maestri (1984)	1	1	2	.333
New York University				
Bill McCarthy (1956)	1	0	2	.000
Larry Geracioti (1969)	1	3	2	.600
North Carolina				
Walt Rabb (1960, 66)	2	0	4	.000
Mike Roberts (1978, 89)	2	2	4	.333
North Carolina State				
Sam Esposito (1968)	1	2	2	.500
Northeastern				
John Connelly (1966)	1	0	2	.000
Northern Colorado				
Pete Butler (1952, 53, 55, 57, 58, 59, 60, 61, 62)	9	2	18	.100
Tom Petrof (1974)	1	1	2	.333

The College World Series Record Book

	Appearances	Won	Lost	Pct.
Notre Dame				
Jake Kline (1957)	1	2	2	.500
Paul Mainieri (2002)	1	1	2	.333
Ohio				
Robert Wren (1970)	1	2	2	.500
Ohio State				
Marty Karow (1951, 65, 66, 67)	4	9	7	.563
Oklahoma				
Jack Baer (1951)	1	4	0	1.000
Enos Semore (1972, 73, 74, 75, 76)	5	5	10	.333
Larry Cochell (1992, 94, 95)	3	5	4	.556
Oklahoma State				
Toby Greene (1954, 55, 59, 60, 61)	5	15	9	.625
Chet Bryan (1966, 67, 68)	3	4	6	.400
Gary Ward (1981, 82, 83, 84, 85, 86, 87 90, 93, 96)	10	19	19	.500
Tom Holliday (1999)	1	0	2	.000
Oral Roberts				
Larry Cochell (1978)	1	1	2	.333
Oregon				
Don Kirsch (1954)	1	0	2	.000
Oregon State				
Ralph Coleman (1952)	1	0	2	.000
Penn State				
Joe Bedenk (1952, 57, 59)	3	7	6	.538
Chuck Medlar (1963, 73)	2	1	4	.200
Pepperdine				
Dave Gorrie (1979)	1	3	2	.600
Andy Lopez (1992)	1	4	0	1.000
Princeton				
Emerson Dickman (1951)	1	0	2	.000
Rice				
Wayne Graham (1997, 99, 02)	2	1	6	.167
Rider				
Tom Petroff (1967)	1	1	2	.333
Rollins				
Joe Justice (1954)	1	3	2	.600
Rutgers				
George Case (1950)	1	3	2	.600

The College World Series Record Book

	Appearances	Won	Lost	Pct.
St. John's (New York)				
Frank McGuire (1949)	1	0	2	.000
Jack Kaiser (1960, 66, 68)	3	5	6	.455
Joe Russo (1978, 80)	2	1	4	.200
St. Louis				
Roy Lee (1965)	1	2	2	.500
San Jose State				
Sam Piraro (2000)	1	0	2	.000
Santa Clara				
Paddy Cottrell (1962)	1	4	2	.667
Seton Hall				
Owen Carroll (1964, 71)	2	1	4	.200
Mike Sheppard (1974, 75)	2	1	4	.200
South Carolina				
Bobby Richardson (1975)	1	4	2	.667
June Raines (1977, 81, 82, 85)	4	5	8	.385
Ray Tanner (2002)	1	4	2	.667
Southern California				
Sam Barry (1948, 49)	2	3	3	.500
Rod Dedeaux (1951, 55, 58, 60, 61, 63 64, 66, 68, 70, 71, 72, 73, 74, 78)	15	60	16	.789
Mike Gillespie (1995, 98, 00, 01)	4	11	7	.611
Southern Illinois				
Joe Lutz (1968, 69)	2	3	4	.429
Richard "Itchy" Jones (1971, 74, 77)	3	9	6	.600
Springfield				
Archie Allen (1951, 55)	2	1	4	.200
Stanford				
Everett Dean (1953)	1	1	2	.333
Dutch Fehring (1967)	1	3	2	.600
Mark Marquess (1982, 83, 85, 87, 88, 90, 95, 97, 99, 00, 01, 02)	11	29	20	.592
Syracuse				
Ted Kleinhans (1961)	1	2	2	.500
Temple				
Skip Wilson (1972, 77)	2	2	4	.333
Tennessee				
S.W. Anderson (1951)	1	4	2	.667
Rod Delmonico (1995, 01)	2	4	4	.500

The College World Series Record Book

	Appearances	Won	Lost	Pct.
Texas				
Bibb Falk (1949, 50, 53, 57, 61 62, 63, 65, 66)	10	20	17	.541
Cliff Gustafson (1968, 69, 70, 72, 73, 74, 75, 79, 81, 82, 83, 84, 85, 87 89, 92, 93)	17	44	30	.595
Augie Garrido (2000, 02)	1	4	2	.667
Texas A&M				
Beau Bell (1951)	1	1	2	.333
Tom Chandler (1964)	1	0	2	.000
Mark Johnson (1993, 99)	2	1	4	.200
Texas-Pan American				
Al Olgletree (1971)	1	2	2	.500
Tufts				
John Ricker (1950)	1	1	2	.333
Tulane				
Rick Jones (2001)	1	1	2	.333
Tulsa				
Gene Shell (1969, 71)	2	6	4	.600
UCLA				
Art Reichle (1969)	1	0	2	.000
Gary Adams (1997)	1	0	2	.000
Utah				
Pete Carlson (1951)	1	2	2	.500
Wake Forest				
Taylor Sanford (1949, 55)	2	7	3	.700
Washington State				
Arthur Bailey (1950, 56)	2	3	4	.429
Bobo Brayton (1965, 76)	2	3	4	.429
Western Michigan				
Charlie Mahr (1952, 55, 58, 59, 61, 63)	6	9	12	.429
Wichita State				
Gene Stephenson (1982, 88, 89, 91, 92, 93, 96)	7	16	11	.593
Wisconsin				
Arthur Mansfield (1950)	1	2	2	.500
Wyoming				
Bud Daniel (1956)	1	1	2	.333
Yale				
Ethan Allen (1947, 48)	2	1	4	.200

The Last Time...

...**a player was awarded first base on catcher's interference:** Greg Schulte, Michigan St. vs. Mississippi State, 5-30-81 (the catcher was Terry Loe)

...**a player was called out for batter's interference:** Brian Barre, Southern California vs. Florida St., 6-14-00

...**a player or coach was ejected from a game:** Rob Klein, first-base coach, Southern California vs. LSU, 7th inning, 6-4-98

...**a player hit a home run to lead-off a game:** Charlton Jimerson, cf, Miami (Fla.) vs. Tennessee, 6-9-01

...**a player hit the first pitch of the game for a home run:** Jason Williams, ss, LSU vs. Wichita St., 6-1-96

...**there were no home runs during a double-header:** Texas vs. Arkansas (13-6) and Stanford vs. Georgia (3-2), 5-30-87.

...**players hit back-to-back-to-back home runs:** Brad Cresse, Clint Earnhart, Wes Davis, LSU vs. Mississippi St., 2nd inning, 6-1-98.

...**a player hit a walk-off homer:** Karl Jernigan, cf, Florida St. vs. Stanford, 6-18-99.

...**a player hit a walk-off homer to end a championship game:** Warren Morris, LSU vs. Miami (Fla.), 6-8-96.

...**a player hit a walk-off grand slam to end an extra-inning game:** Paul Carey, Stanford vs. LSU, 6-5-87.

...**a player hit a pinch-hit home run:** Eddie Davis, ph-lf, Long Beach State vs. LSU, 6-9-93 (10-8).

...**a player hit a pinch-hit home run to end a 9-inning game:** Dave Shermet, Arizona vs. Maine, 5-30-86.

...**a pitcher earned the win and hit a home run in the same game:** Jason Lane, Southern California vs. Arizona State, 6-6-98.

...**a player was called out for using an illegal bat:** Tony Barquin, Miami (Fla.) vs. Michigan, 6-2-80.

...**a game featured two complete games by the starting pitcher:** Jonathan Johnson, Florida State vs. Mark Redman, Oklahoma, 6-2-95.

...**pitchers threw a combined shutout:** Tim Dixon & Mark Chavez, Cal State Fullerton vs. Tennessee, 6-8-95.

a pitcher threw nine innings of relief in a 9-inning game: Dic Larner, California vs. Yale, 6-27-47.

...**a pitcher also played catcher in the same game:** Gettys Glaze, Citadel vs. Cal State Fullerton, 6-4-90.

...**a pitcher threw a complete-game shutout:** Brad Rigby, Georgia Tech vs. Cal State Fullerton, 6-3-94.

...**a player tossed a live ball into the stands as a souvenir:** Gary Burnham, Clemson vs. Miami (Fla.), 5-31-96 (Rudy Gomez hit a ball down the third-base line and Burnham, thinking it was foul, tossed the ball into the stands and Gomez was awarded home)

...**a game was shortened because of rain:** South Carolina vs. Eastern Michigan, 6 innings.

...**a team hit three home runs in one inning:** LSU vs. Mississippi State, 6-1-98.

...**a tornado warning evacuated the press box:** 6-13-00.

...**both benches left the dugout:** La.-Lafayette vs. Clemson, 6-14-00.

...**a team lost its first game and came back to win the championship:** Southern California, 1998

The College World Series Record Book

National Championship Totals

TEAM	TITLES
Southern California	12 (48, 58, 61, 63, 69, 70, 71, 72, 73, 74, 78, 98)
Arizona State	5 (65, 67, 69, 77, 81)
LSU	5 (91, 93, 96, 97, 00)
Texas	5 (49, 50, 75, 83, 02)
Miami (Fla.)	4 (82, 85, 99, 01)
Arizona	3 (76, 80, 86)
Cal State Fullerton	3 (79, 84, 95)
Minnesota	3 (56, 60, 64)
California	2 (47, 57)
Michigan	2 (53, 62)
Oklahoma	2 (51, 94)
Stanford	2 (87, 88)
Georgia	1 (90)
Holy Cross	1 (52)
Missouri	1 (54)
Ohio State	1 (66)
Oklahoma State	1 (59)
Pepperdine	1 (92)
Wake Forest	1 (55)
Wichita State	1 (89)

The 1958 Trojans took home the second College World Series title for Southern California, which has won a dozen national championships.

The 1972 Florida Southern players show off their individual awards. The Moccasins have won eight Division II College World Series. (Photo courtesy of Florida Southern.)

The 2002 Columbus State Cougars pile on after winning the 2002 national championship. (Photo courtesy of Mike Peacock and Columbus State.)

Division II Records

Division II Results, 1968-2002

Year	Champion (Record)	Coach	Score	Runner-up
1968	Chapman (35-18)	Paul Deese	11-0	Delta St.
1969	Illinois St (33-5)	Duffy Bass	12-0	SW Missouri St.
1970	Cal St. Northridge (41-21)	Bob Hiegert	2-1	Nicholls St.
1971	Fla. Southern (34-4)	Hal Smeltzly	4-0	Central Michigan
1972	Fla. Soutern (31-6)	Hal Smeltzly	5-1	Cal St. Northridge
1973	UC Irvine (44-12)	Gary Adams	9-6	Ithaca
1974	UC Irvine (48-8)	Gary Adams	14-1	New Orleans
1975	Fla. Southern (35-10)	Hal Smeltzly	10-7	Marietta
1976	Cal Poly Pomona (40-27-1)	John Scolinos	17-3	SIU-Edwardsville
1977	UC Riverside (43-19)	Jack Smitheran	4-1	Eckerd
1978	Fla. Southern (41-8)	Joe Arnold	7-2	Delta St.
1979	Valdosta St. (47-14)	Tommy Thomas	3-2	Fla. Southern
1980	Cal Poly Pomona (42-25-1)	John Scolinos	13-6	New Haven
1981	Fla. Southern (55-8)	Joe Arnold	9-0	Eastern Ill.
1982	UC Riverside (36-23)	Jack Smitheran	10-1	Fla. Southern
1983	Cal Poly Pomona (41-22)	John Scolinos	9-7	Jacksonville St.
1984	Cal St. Northridge (46-21-1)	Bob Hiegert	10-5	Fla. Southern
1985	Fla. Southern (54-10)	Chuck Anderson	15-5	Cal Poly Pomona
1986	Troy St. (46-8)	Chase Riddle	5-0	Columbus St.
1987	Troy St. (38-10-1)	Chase Riddle	7-5	Tampa
1988	Fla. Southern (48-10)	Chuck Anderson	5-4	Cal St Sacramento
1989	Cal Poly (38-25)	Steve McFarland	9-5	New Haven
1990	Jacksonville St. (43-9)	Rudy Abbott	12-8	Cal St. Northridge
1991	Jacksonville St. (41-12)	Rudy Abbott	20-4	Mo. Southern St.
1992	Tampa (42-19)	Lelo Prado	11-8	Mansfield
1993	Tampa (43-21)	Lelo Prado	7-5	Cal Poly
1994	Central Mo. St. (51-11)	Dave Van Horn	14-9	Fla. Southern
1995	Fla. Southern (51-10)	Chuck Anderson	15-0	Georgia C&SU
1996	Kennesaw St. (48-17)	Mike Sansing	4-0	St. Joseph's (Ind.)
1997	Cal St. Chico (52-11)	Lindsay Meggs	13-12	Central Oklahoma
1998	Tampa (46-14)	Terry Rupp	6-1	Kennesaw St.
1999	Cal St. Chico (50-17)	Lindsay Meggs	11-5	Kennesaw St.
2000	Southeastern Okla. (43-12)	Mike Metheny	7-2	Fort Hays St.
2001	St. Mary's (Texas) (50-13)	Charlie Migl	11-3	Cenral Mo. St
2002	Columbus St.	Greg Appleton	5-3	Chico State

Most Outstanding Player Award

1968 Tony Spono, of, Chapman
1969 Tom Klein, 1b, Illinois State
1970 Chuck Stone, of, Cal State Northridge

1971	Greg Pryor, 2b, and Kevin Bryant, 3b, Florida Southern
1972	Jay Smith, p, Florida Southern
1973	Terry Stupy, c, UC Irvine
1974	Jeff Malinoff, 2b, UC Irvine
1975	Joe Yazombek, c, Marietta
1976	Ken Hellyer, of, Cal Poly Pomona
1977	Joe Lefebvre, of-p, Ekerd and Steve Glaum, p, UC Riverside
1978	Ricky Perkins, 3b, Delta State
1979	Frank DeGennaro, of, Valdosta State
1980	Brian Zell, of, Cal Poly Pomona
1981	Joe Sickles, of, Florida Southern
1982	Joe Sickles, of, Florida Southern
1983	Larry Beardman, of, Cal Poly Pomona
1984	Perry Husband, 2b, Cal State Northridge
1985	Tom Temrowski, 2b, Florida Southern
1986	Wendell Stephens, 3b, Troy State
1987	Jude Rinaldi, 1b, Troy State
1988	Chris Leach, of, Florida Southern
1989	Steve DiBartolomeo, p, New Haven
1990	Tim Van Egmond, p, Jacksonville State
1991	Tim Van Egmond, p, Jacksonville State
1992	Joe Urso, 2b, Tampa
1993	David Dion, of, Tampa
1994	James Vida, 1b, Florida Southern
1995	Brett Tomko, p, Florida Southern
1996	Chris Halliday, c, Kennesaw State
1997	Angel Diaz, c, Tampa
1998	Ronnie Merrill, ss, Tampa
1999	John-Eric Hernandez, p, Cal State Chico
2000	Aaron Thompson, p, Southeastern Oklahoma
2001	Jesse Gutierrez, 1b, St. Mary's (Texas)
2002	Brian Barker, p, Columbus State

DIVISION II RECORDS
INDIVIDUAL RECORDS

At Bats
8 - by three players (last time: Blake Rosson, North Ala. (9) vs. Grand Valley St. (10), 5-18-85)

Runs
6 - Tom Michalak, Lewis (27) vs. Ferris St.(2), 5-18-90.

Hits
6 - by four players (last time: Bill Petko, West Virginia St. (15) vs. West

Liberty State (7), 5-15-98).
Doubles
  4 - Ruben Ayala, UC Riverside (12) vs. Jacksonville St. (10), 5-30-91
Triples
  2 - by several
Home Runs
  4 - Jamie Detillon, Ashland (11) vs. Quincy (10), 5-16-99
Runs Batted In
  9 - by four players (last time: Jeff Gordon, Tampa (17), vs. Florida Southern (19), 5-19-95)
Total Bases
  16 - Jamie Detillon, Ashland (11) vs. Quincy (10), 5-16-99
Stolen Bases
  4 - by two players (last time: Pierre Gomez, Norfolk St. (6) vs. Ky. Wesleyan (12), 5-20-88)

PITCHING
SINGLE GAME

Innings Pitched
  15 - by two pitchers (last time: Steve Wendell, Quinnipiac (1) vs. Mansfield (3), 5-21-88)
Most Hits Allowed
  19 - by two players (last time: Greg Valentini, West Georgia (28) vs. Slippery Rock (8), 5-14-82)
Fewest Hits Allowed (Complete Game)
  0 - by three pitchers (last time: Steve Charles, Troy St. (5) vs. Mansfield (0), 5-29-93)
Runs Allowed
  14, by two players (last time: Chad Danielson, South Dakota St. (10) vs. Central Mo. St. (15), 5-20-95)
Earned Runs Allowed
  13 - Chad Danielson, South Dakota St. (10) vs. Central Mo. St. (15), 5-20-95
Strikeouts
  20 - Ted Barnicle, Jacksonville St. (2) vs. Southeastern La. (5), 5-16,75
Bases on Balls
  12 - Robby Glisson, Chapman (15) vs. Cal St. Northridge (12), 5-18-84

FIELDING
SINGLE GAME

Putouts
  24 - Doug Bond, Quinnipiac (1) vs. Mansfield (3), 5-21-88.
Assists
  11 - by two players (last time: Jimmy Lester, Columbus St. (19) vs. Longwood (1), 5-17-84)

Errors
5 - Mike Vargo, Tampa (17) vs. Fla. Southern (19), 5-19-95.

TEAM RECORDS
BATTING
SINGLE GAME

At Bats
58 - Lewis (27) vs. Ferris St. (2), 5-18-90
Runs
29 - Florida Southern vs. Florida Atlantic (11), 5-16-85
Runs, One Inning
14 - SIU-Edwardsville vs. Adelphi (4), second inning, 5-26-97
Hits
30 - by two teams (last time: Lewis (27) vs. Ferris St. (2), 5-18-90)
Doubles
10 - Wright St. (26) vs. Youngstown St. (1), 5-19-77
Triples
5 - South Dakota St. (13) vs. Northwest Mo. St. (1), 5-18-73
Home Runs
8 - by two teams (last time: Longwood (11) vs. Shippensburg (15), 5-14-92)
Runs Batted In
27, by two teams (last time: Florida Southern (29) vs. Florida Atlantic (11), 5-16-85)
Total Bases
54 - Lewis (24) vs. Sam Houston St. (8), 5-18-84
Left on Base
19 - New Orleans (6) vs. Nicolls St. (10), 5-24-74

PITCHING

Strikeouts, One Game
20 - Jacksonville St. (2) vs. Southwestern La. (5), 5-16-75
Bases on Balls, One Game
16 - by two teams (last time: Mesa St. (13) vs. Sonoma St. (17), 5-14-99)
Consecutive Shutout Innings
21 - Fla. Southern (9 innings vs. Old Dominion, 5-25-72; 21, 9 innings vs. Montclair St., 5-26-72; 3 innings vs. New Haven, 5-27-72)

FIELDING

Assists
26 - by two teams (last time: Quinnipiac (1) vs. Mansfield (3), 5-21-88)
Errors
11 - by three teams (last time: Minn. St.-Mankato (7) vs. Lewis (14), 5-17-86)
Double Plays
6 - Tampa (5) vs. West Ga. (1), 5-25-98.

The College World Series Record Book

Boxscore for
National Championship Final 2002

May 28, 2002

Columbus State	ab	r	h	rbi	Chico State	ab	r	h	rbi
Chris Gilstrap ss	5	1	1	0	Robby Poole 2b	4	0	0	1
Josh Maner 2b	4	0	0	0	Jeff Walker cf	4	0	0	0
Ladd Hammond 3b	4	1	1	1	Steve Newson rf	5	0	2	0
Andrew Ginther c	2	0	0	0	John Moylan dh	4	0	0	0
Taylor Groce lf	4	2	3	3	Rusty Kawachi c	4	0	1	0
Jay Bayer dh	4	1	2	1	Ryan Tash 3b	3	2	0	0
Brian Koon rf	4	0	0	0	Miguel Mendoza lf	4	1	1	0
Chad Mcconnell pr/rf	0	0	0	0	Ryan Wulfert 1b	3	0	1	1
Ben Sutter 1b	3	0	0	0	Rich Janeway ph	1	0	1	0
Shawn Sewell cf	4	0	1	0	Johnny Molina ss	3	0	1	0
					Jimmy Lintt ph	0	0	0	1
Totals	34	5	8	5	Totals	35	3	8	3

Columbus State 100 021 001 - 5 8 2
Chico State   010 000 002 - 3 8 2

E-Hammond, Sewell, Wulfert 2. LOB-Cougars 5; Wildcats 9. 2B-Gilstrap, Newsom 2. HR-Groce 2, Bayer. HBP-Ginther, Sutter, Poole, Tash. SH-Walker. SF-Lintt. CS-Ginther.

	IP	H	R	ER	BB	SO
Columbus State						
Jason Burdette (W, 11-2)	9	8	3	2	0	3
Chico State						
Adam Montarbo (L, 12-3)	6	5	4	4	1	1
David Goni	.1	1	0	0	0	0
Brian Thomas	2	0	1	1	1	0
Dale Thayer	.2	1	0	0	0	1

HB-Burdette 2, Montarbo, Thomas. Umpires-Jay DeSantis, Thomas Quackenbush, Ricky Armstrong, Chris Coskey. T-2:35. A-1,653.

2002 ALL-TOURNAMENT TEAM

c - Matt Tupman, UMass Lowell
1b - Michael Regan, UMass Lowell
2b - Josh Maner, Columbus State
3b - Ladd Hammond, Columbus State
ss - Chris Gilstrap, Columbus State
of - Steve Newson, Chico State
of - Shawn Sewell, Columbus State
of - Taylor Groce, Columbus State
dh - Jeff Walker, Chico State
p - Brian Baker, Columbus State
p - Jason Burdette, Columbus State

A Columbus State pitcher lets one rip. (Photo courtesy of Mike Peacock and Columbus State.)

The College World Series Record Book

National Championship Totals

TEAM	TITLES
Florida Southern	8 (71, 72, 75, 78, 81, 85, 88, 95)
Cal Poly Pomona	3 (76, 80, 83)
Tampa	3 (92, 93, 98)
Cal State Chico	2 (97, 99)
Cal State Northridge	2 (70, 84)
Jacksonville State	2 (90, 91)
Troy State	2 (86, 87)
UC Irvine	2 (73, 74)
UC Riverside	2 (77, 82)
Cal Poly	1 (89)
Central Missouri State	1 (94)
Chapman	1 (68)
Columbus State	1 (02)
Kennesaw State	1 (96)
Illinois State	1 (69)
Southeastern Oklahoma	1 (00)
St. Mary's (Texas)	1 (01)
Valdosta State	1 (79)

World Series Sites

1968-72	Springfield, Missouri
1973-79	Springfield, Illinois
1980-84	Riverside, California
1985-02	Montgomery, Alabama

The Florida Southern Moccasins won the 1978 Division II national championship.

Hitters get ready to take their turn at bat during the Division III College World Series.

Eastern Connecticut players run on the field after winning the Division III College World Series in 2002.

The College World Series Record Book

Division III Records

Division III Results, 1976-2002

Year	Champion (Record)	Coach	Score	Runner-up
1976	Cal St. Stanislaus (33-20-2)	Jim Bowen	13-6	Ithaca
1977	Cal St. Stanislaus (33-18-1)	Jim Bowen	8-5	Brandeis
1978	Rowan (29-11)	Michael Briglia	5-3	Marietta
1979	Rowan (29-5)	Michael Briglia	3-0	Cal St. Stanislaus
1980	Ithaca (33-4)	George Valesente	12-5	Marietta
1981	Marietta (59-5)	Dan Schaly	14-12	Ithaca
1982	Eastern Conn. St (38-6-1)	Bill Holowaty	11-6	Cal St. Stanislaus
1983	Marietta (49-9)	Don Schaly	36-8	Otterbein
1984	Ramapo (35-11)	Mickey Ennis	5-4	Marietta
1985	Wis.-Oshkosh (37-3)	Russ Tiedemann	11-6	Marietta
1986	Marietta (48-13-2)	Don Schaly	11-6	Ithaca
1987	Montclair St. (34-14-1)	Kevin Cooney	13-12	Wis.-Oshkosh
1988	Ithaca (36-4-1)	George Valesente	7-5	Wis.-Oshkosh
1989	N.C. Wesleyan (33-11-1)	Mike Fox	8-7	Cal St. Stanislaus
1990	Eastern Conn. St. (40-6)	Bill Holowaty	8-1	Aurora
1991	Southern Me. (38-6)	Ed Flaherty	9-0	Col. of New Jersey
1992	Wm. Paterson (36-7)	Jeff Albies	3-1	Cal Lutheran
1993	Montclair St. (37-11)	Norm Schoenig	3-1	Wis.-Oshkosh
1994	Wis.-Oshkosh (41-4)	Tom Lechnir	6-2	Wesleyan (Conn.)
1995	La Verne (39-9)	Owen Wright	5-3	Methodist
1996	Wm. Paterson (39-5-1)	Jeff Albies	6-5	Cal Lutheran
1997	Southern Me. (39-9)	Ed Flaherty	15-1	Wooster
1998	Eastern Conn. St. (40-11)	Bill Holowaty	16-1	Montclair St.
1999	N.C. Wesleyan (42-9)	Charle Long	1-0	St. Thomas (Minn.)
2000	Montclair St. (42-6-1)	Norm Schoeing	6-2	St. Thomas (Minn.)
2001	St. Thomas (Minn.) (39-10)	Dennis Denning	8-4	Marietta
2002	East. Conn. St. (39-11-1)	Bill Holowaty	8-0	Marietta

Most Outstanding Player

1976	Dan Boer, 1b, Cal State Stanislaus
1977	Rusty Kuntz, of, Cal State Stanislaus
1978	Bob Pfeffer, p, Rowan
1979	Tak Upshur, 2b, Rowan
1980	John Nicholo, ss, Ithaca
1981	John Schaly, 2b, Marietta
1982	Jeff Blobaum, p, Cal State Stanislaus
1983	Jim Pancher, 2b, Marietta
1984	Derek Bastinck, c, Ramapo
1985	Terry Jorgensen, lf, Wisconsin-Oskosh
1986	Mike Brandts, 3b, Marietta

1987 John Deutsch, rf, Montclair State
1988 Joe Sottolano, p, Ithaca
1989 James Anderson, 1b, North Carolina Wesleyan
1990 Brian Mercado, dh, Eastern Connecticut State
1991 Gary Williamson, of, Southern Maine
1992 Ralph Perdomo, 1b, William Paterson
1993 Drew Yocum, p, Montclair State
1994 Tim Jorgensen, ss, Wisconsin-Oshkosh
1995 Jeff Polinsky, 1b, La Verne
1996 Mark DeMenna, of, William Paterson
1997 Jason Jensen, p, Southern Maine
1998 Chris D'Amato, 2b, Eastern Connecticut State
1999 Barry Blake, ss, North Carolina Wesleyan
2000 Corey Hamman, p, Montclair State
2001 Brad Bonine, of, St. Thomas of Minnesota
2002 John Kubachka, 1b, Eastern Conn. State

DIVISION III RECORDS
BATTING - SINGLE GAME

At-Bats
8 - by three players (last time: Jason Lensmeyer, Carthage (10) vs. Monmouth (Ill.) (8), 5-18-2002)

Runs
6 - by four players (last time: Bob Prince, Southern Me. (21) vs. Mass-Dartmouth (4), 6-16-91)

Hits
6 - by four players (last time: Jeff Zappa, Wis.-Oskhosh (21) vs. St. Thomas (Minn.) (10), 5-18-96)

Doubles
4 - Mark Murray, Claremont-M-S (17) vs. Cal Luthern (4), 5-16-96

Triples
3 - Greg Clark, N.C. Wesleyan (27) vs. Upsala (9), 5-18-81

Home Runs
4 - by two players (last time: Dave Kennedy, Montclair St. (19) vs. St. Lawrence (11), 5-16-91)

Runs Batted In
8 - by several (last time: Scott Baron, Aurora (22) vs. Wartburg (11), 5-16-97).

Total Bases
17 - by two players (last time: Dave Kennedy, Montclair St. (19) vs. St. Lawrence (11), 5-16-91)

Stolen Bases
5 - Rich McNeill, Methodist (16) vs. Salisbury St. (8), 5-22-83

PITCHING

Innings Pitched
13 - Danny Tester, Methodist (2) vs. Cal St. Stanislaus (1), 6-3-88

Most Hits Allowed
17 - by four players (last time: Bryan Toor, St. Thomas (Minn.) (3) vs. Montclair St. (13), 5-30-00)

No Hitters
1 - Norm Charlesworth, Rowan (4) vs. Johns Hopkins (1), 5-15-80

Runs Allowed
15 - Chris Morgan, Ripon (4) vs. Carthage (15), 5-19-99

Earned Runs Allowed
14 - Glen Alexander, Otterbein (8) vs. Marietta (36), 6-7-83

Strikeouts
19 - Matt DeSalvo, Marietta (1) vs. Salisbury (0), 5-25-01

Bases on Balls
11 - by three players (last time: Mike Bolson, Wis.-Whitewater (6) vs. Benedictine (Ill.) (5), 5-19-00)

FIELDING

Putouts
21 - Aaron Missler, Ohio Wesleyan (10) vs. Rose-Hulman (2), 5-16-96.

Assists
11 - by two players (last time: Mike Royer, Ohio Wesleyan (2) vs. Benedictine (Ill.) (3), 5-16-91)

Errors
6 - Kevin Creehan, Allegheny (15) vs. Marietta (19), 5-19-96

TEAM RECORDS
SINGLE GAME - BATTING

At-Bats
62 - Carthage (10) vs. Monmouth (Ill.) (7), 5-18-02.

Runs
36 - Marrieta vs. Otterbein (8) 6-7-83; Wis.-Oskosh vs. Wis.-Whitewater (10), 5-16-89

Runs, One Inning
18 - Cal St. San B'dino (31) vs. Redlands (5), first inning, 5-18-91

Hits
33 - Marietta (36) vs. Otterbein (8), 6-7-83

Doubles
10 - by two teams (last time: Upper Iowa (18) vs. MacMurray (5), 5-18-96)

Triples
4 - by two teams (last time: N.C. Wesleyan (17) vs. Otterbein (4), 6-4-83)

Home Runs
8 - Wis.-Oskosh (36) vs. Wis.-Whitewater (10), 4-26-89
RBI
36 - Marietta (36) vs. Otterbein (8), 6-7-83
Total Bases
57 - Wis.-Oskosh (36) vs. Wis.-Whitewater (10), 5-26-89
Left on Base
19 - Baldwin-Wallace (8) vs. Marietta (12), 5-26-88
Stolen Bases
9 - by two teams (last time: Methodist (8) vs. Rensselaer (7), 5-23-96)

PITCHING

Strikeouts, One Game
18 - by three teams (last time: N.C. Wesleyan (4) vs. Chapman (3) (13 inn.), 5-25-97)
Bases on Balls Allowed, One Game
19 - Marietta (6) vs. Ithaca (5), 5-29-81; Otterbein (8) vs. Marietta (36), 6-7-83
Consecutive Shutout Innings
23 - Chapman, 5-27-00 vs. Southern Me. (eight inn.); 5-28-00 vs. Cortland St. (nine inn.); 5-29-00 vs. St. Thomas (Minn.) (six inn.)
Pitchers Used
8 - Methodist (3) vs. Southern Me. (12), 5-27-91

FIELDING

Assists
29 - Salisbury St. (9) vs. N.C. Wesleyan (8), 5-19-00.
Errors
11 - Wooster (7) vs. North Park (13), 5-27-88
Double Plays
5 - by many (last time: Southern Me. (6) vs. Williams, 5-20-01).

World Series Sites

1976-87	Marietta, Ohio
1988--89	Bristol, Connecticut
1990-94	Battle Creek, Michigan
1995-1999	Salem, Virginia
2000-2002	Appleton, Wisconsin

The College World Series Record Book

Boxscore for
2002 National Championship Final 2002
May 28, 2002

Eastern Connecticut	ab	r	h	rbi	Marietta	ab	r	h	rbi
Morgan Thompson 2b	5	1	1	1	Chris Sidick cf	4	0	0	0
Justin Waz dh	5	2	4	3	Todd Yoder dh	4	0	1	0
Dwight Wildman cf	5	0	1	1	Brent Curtin 3b	3	0	0	0
John Kubachka 1b	5	1	3	1	Jay Coakley c	2	0	0	0
John Hedde lf	5	0	0	0	Kevin May 1b	4	0	1	0
Jared Holowaty rf	4	1	1	0	Matt McLuckey rf	4	0	1	0
Inaki Ormaechea 3b	4	1	1	0	Derek Pauley lf	4	0	2	0
Tom Koch ss	4	0	2	0	Dusty Childress 2b	4	0	0	0
Jeff Funaro c	4	2	1	0	Nate Brown ss	3	0	0	0
Totals	41	8	14	6	Totals	32	0	5	0

Eastern Connecticut   050 010 002 - 8 14 1
Marietta College   000 000 000 - 0   4 1

E-Thompson, Childress. DP - Eastern Connecticut 1. LOB-Eastern Connecticut 6, Marietta 8. 2B-Waz 2, Pauley. 3B-Waz. CS-Koch

	IP	H	R	ER	BB	SO
Eastern Connecticut						
Joey Serfass (W, 10-1)	9	5	0	0	2	6
Marietta						
Trey Lamb (L, 9-2)	9	14	8	3	0	9

HBP-by Serfass (Curtin). Umpires-Geroge Drouches, John Ramsey, Jim Jackson, Rod Murphy. T-1:57. A-988.

All-Tournament Team

p - Justin Papania, Marietta College
p - Joey Serfass, Eastern Connecticut
p - Scott Stocker, Marietta College
1b - John Kubachka, Eastern Connecticut
1b - Colin Renick, College of New Jersey
1b - Dan Quinn, Rensselaer Polytechnic Institute
3b - Chris Phaup, Christopher Newport U.
of - John Hedde, Eastern Connecticut
of - Chris Sidick, Marietta College
utility - Travis Teeter, Rensselaer Polytechnic Institute
dh - Justin Waz, Eastern Connecticut

The College World Series Record Book

National Championship Totals

TEAM	TITLES
Eastern Connecticut State	4 (82, 90, 98, 02)
Cal State Stanislaus	2 (76, 77)
Ithaca	2 (80, 88)
Marietta	2 (81, 83)
Montclair State	2 (87, 93)
N.C. Wesleyan	2 (89, 99)
Rowan	2 (78, 79)
Southern Maine	2 (91, 97)
William Patterson	2 (92, 96)
Wisconsin-Oshkosh	2 (85, 94)
La Verne	1 (95)
Ramapo	1 (84)
St. Thomas (Minn.)	1 (01)

Eastern Connecticut players hold up their winning plaque.

The College World Series Record Book

Survey

Please take the following survey, the results of which will be used in the next edition of the book.

What Division I players do you feel were the best at their position between 1996-2003?

p _____

p _____

1b _____

2b _____

ss _____

3b _____

of _____

of _____

of _____

dh _____

What Division I players do you feel were the best during the entire length of the College World Series (1947-2003)?

p _____

p _____

1b _____

2b _____

ss _____

3b _____

of _____

of _____

of _____

dh _____

What teams do you feel were the best ever in CWS history?

Division I _____

Division II _____

Division III _____

If you want to be on our mail list, please complete the following:

Name _____

Address _____

City, State, Zip _____

Tear this page out of the book or copy and mail to: Madden Publishing Company, 10872 Washington Bay Drive, Fishers, IN 46038. To order the next edition of the book, send $12.95 by check or money order to the Madden Publishing.